971
.104
0924
Benne-K

Keene, Roger.
    Conversations with W.A.C. Bennett;
based on a series of interviews conducted
by Roger Keene. Background scenario by
David C. Humphreys. Toronto, Methuen,
1980.
    xii, 146 p. ill.
    Bibliography: p. 144.

1. Bennett, William Andrew Cecil, 1900-1979.
2. Prime ministers - British Columbia -
Biography.
                (Continued on next card)
0458943002   1026127

6/he

Conversations With
W.A.C.
BENNETT

Conversations With
W.A.C.
BENNETT

Based on a series of interviews conducted by
Roger Keene
Background scenario by
David C. Humphreys

ⓝ Methuen

Toronto New York London Sydney

Cover photo: Peter Paterson

Canadian Cataloguing in Publication Data

Keene, Roger.
    Conversations with W.A.C. Bennett

Bibliography: p.
Includes index.
ISBN 0-458-94300-2

1. Bennett, William A.C., 1900–1979.   2. Prime
ministers - British Columbia - Biography.
3. British Columbia - Politics and government -
1952-1975.* I. Bennett, William A.C., 1900–1979.
II. Humphreys, David C., 1938–   III. Title.

FC3827.1.B46K43   971.1′04′0924   C80-094212-4
F1088.B46K43

Printed and bound in Canada

1 2 3 4 5   80   81 82 83 84

Contents

Acknowledgments

With thanks to Linda Humphreys, Catherine Marfleet, Digby Peers, and The Honourable Donald Phillips, for help and support at various stages.

The authors also are grateful to the following for providing photographic material for this book: Mrs. Russell (Connie) Bennett who was kind enough to loan us several pictures from her private collection; British Columbia Hydro and Power Authority; British Columbia Provincial Government; Kings County Museum, Hampton, New Brunswick; Marshall–Wells Company, Edmonton; Ms. Fern Miller, Toronto; National Photography Collection, Public Archives, Canada; NFB Phototheque ONF © Ottawa; Provincial Archives of British Columbia, and the Vancouver *Province*.

Foreword

I met "Wacky" Bennett's three immediate predecessors, premiers "Boss" Johnson, John Hart and T. D. Pattullo, before I met him—indeed before I had ever heard of him. It was soon after Newfoundland had become a province of Canada with me as its premier. The meeting is vivid in my memory; it was a purely social occasion in "Boss" Johnson's residence along the shore outside Victoria.

Perhaps it was because I knew Mr. Bennett over a much longer period of time that I got to know him better than his predecessors but, and this may be a superficial judgment, the fact remains that he persists in my mind as a stronger personality than those three put together.

When Bennett and I exchanged compliments at a federal-provincial conference in Ottawa, he describing extravagantly his and British Columbia's goodwill for Newfoundland, and I telling the conference that the leaders and people of British Columbia had always given voice to cordial feelings toward Newfoundland, the exchange brought a smiling comment from Lester Pearson who quipped, "Canada's book-ends!" I, so conscious of Bennett's vehement opposition to the very federal philosophy of equalization payments to the have-not provinces, without which they could scarcely function in Confederation, agreed with Pearson, "Yes, book-ends holding three books, a chequebook in British Columbia and Eaton's and Simpson's catalogues in Newfoundland."

About 4,000 miles of Canadian soil separated Premier Bennett and me, but far longer was the philosophical, ideological and partisan distance between us. We had diametrically different concepts of Canada, of Confederation and of Canadian unity. On one memorable occasion he and I successfully debated the matter in a CBC national broadcast. He was at his best, and in that debate he eloquently foreshadowed the very spirit of René Lévesque's doctrine.

But the interesting fact is that we shared so thoroughly a

technique of government. He overlapped twenty of my twenty-three years in office, and this fascinating book could be an account of my efforts in Newfoundland and Labrador. When Bennett spoke of his term in office he said, "We had a great hydro system, great universities, medicare, highways, everything, all had been completed."

I have read *Conversations With W.A.C. Bennett*, every word and syllable of it, with pleasure. I am so glad that it was written.

Hon. Joseph R. Smallwood

Preface

This book is based upon a series of interviews with W. A. C. Bennett, conducted one and a half years before his death. The interviewer was Roger Keene. It was the second time the two men had met—their paths had first crossed during the campaign for the 1972 British Columbia election. Keene, then a television news director, saw it as his job to make the most of one of the few interviews the premier had agreed to give. What followed was an adversary interview, with a winner and a loser. Keene admits that the aging premier won, if not the election, at least that round in his campaign.

When the dust had settled, and Bennett had lost the election, Keene knew that much of the Bennett story was still untold. W. A. C. Bennett had guided British Columbia through its transition from one of Canada's most backward regions to one of the world's most prosperous. Yet, Bennett had no plans to write his memoirs. As a result, future generations would have only third-person interpretations of his life. With this in mind, Keene contacted him again. Bennett agreed to tell, on tape, the story of his life.

Over a three and a half week period in 1977, the two men sat down together. Bennett was no longer an active politician. He now enjoyed telling the tales he would not earlier have told, of the machinations and manoeuvres which are part of holding power for twenty years. Keene was pleased with the tapings, and so was Bennett.

Roger Keene took the tapes to David C. Humphreys, an award-winning radio producer and writer. Humphreys had made his mark with radio biographies of such luminaries as Bertrand Russell and Bertolt Brecht. At first, he saw little similarity between W. A. C. Bennett and the legendary figures whose lives he had documented. But after listening to the tapes, he changed his mind. Bennett's life, he realized, was as much a saga as any he had dramatized on radio. He agreed to provide material that would create a background for a book on Bennett's life.

This is that book. It is a happy tale; the story of a man who enjoyed his personal life and his extraordinary political career.

Introduction

My father was not a mysterious or complex man, as some have said, but rather, a strong, caring man dedicated to the well-being and future of all Canadians and particularly the people of British Columbia. He insisted that his private life be left out of the public eye. He taught his children at a very early age the value of work and commitment—and, by example, created the feeling of well-being and happiness that comes from a good family life.

To the very end of his life, my father never lost his sense of humour or his ability and love of debate. He always encouraged his family to enter into discussions and voice opinions on any subject we wished during family dinners or family times.

W. A. C. loved his country and his fellow men and women. He counted among his many friends people from all walks of life, from varied religious and ethnic backgrounds, and from political parties other than his own.

On leaving Government House after giving Lieutenant-Governor, the Honourable John Nicholson his government's resignation after their defeat in 1972, His Honour, I believe, echoed the sentiment of political friend and foe alike by saying—"Thank you for a job well done."

Premier Bill Bennett

"Government and business are simple. It's only people who make them complicated. They call a conference for this, and another one for that. They write memos to cover up what they do not know. As a rule, the bigger the business or the government, the less efficient it will be."

"Hornets meet hornets, flies meet flies, birds of a feather flock together, and the same goes for newsmen. They meet at the Press Club, for lunch, all talking the same stuff. They start to believe their own propaganda."

"If you have six or seven problems on your mind all at once, then you are not thinking, you are worrying. But if you write them down one by one and concentrate on them one at a time, the solution will come easily. I'm a hardware merchant. We sell rope, thick rope that you cannot break. But, if you take each strand separately, you can break the rope in a few minutes."

"Nobody can rise, unless it's against criticism. Even a kite can't rise with the wind, it's got to go against it."

W. A. C. BENNETT

~ 1 ~

Early Days

I REMEMBER my early days in New Brunswick, a boy brought
up in a very poor home, running around with bare feet in
the summertime, hair clipped short so that I could go swim-
ming and have fun. To think that this young lad would someday be premier of British Columbia makes me laugh. I think
that's a very good joke.

The Appalachian Mountains rise in southern Georgia, rearing
lush slopes and pitching down into deep, secretive valleys until
the chain dies on the plains of New Brunswick, falling toward
the Atlantic Ocean. The greenness of these mountains is decep-
tive, for the soil is thin and liable to run-offs in the heavy spring
rain. The man who farms here earns little but heartbreak and a
bare subsistence. But the streams and rivers that carry off his
soil turn the wheels of mills, and it is in those narrow-windowed
buildings that he earns the money that keeps his family from
hunger. This pattern of life holds true in the Carolinas, in the
Virginias and in Albert County, New Brunswick, bordering
Chignecto Bay.

Hastings in Albert County is where William Andrew Cecil
was born on September 6, 1900. His father, Andrew, farmed
there and worked in the nearby mill. Times were hard in Hastings and a move to nearby Hampton produced no better result
for the family's standard of living.

It was fortunate that Cecil's mother, Emma Burns Bennett,
came from hard and frugal Presbyterian stock. She saw to it that
the family never lacked for basic food, clothing and cleanliness.
She kept a spotless house and an impeccable Sabbath. Religion

1

was the central thread in the fabric of the Bennett household, and the habits and observances impressed upon him by his mother remained with Cecil Bennett for the rest of his life.

Outside the house, another force held sway. This was politics. There were still many in the province who remembered Confederation, when the Maritimes had passed into union with central Canada, and there were many who regretted the act. There were others who sympathized with their cousins in New England who, at this time, were striking the cotton mills and clashing with the militia. Life in New Brunswick tilted on a north–south axis anyway, despite Confederation with the Canadas. Friends and relatives were to be found in Maine and Massachusetts. Rare was the New Brunswicker who had kinfolk in Ontario or Quebec. New Brunswick was a land out of kilter with its past, swaying toward a new equilibrium—fruitful ground for high political passion.

The Bennetts did not hold with those who looked to the Boston States as home. Nor did they sympathize with the radicals, the mill-burners. They were conservative folk, both by conviction and party vote. They believed in the Canada of Sir John A. Macdonald as they believed in the Crown. Their ancestors had left the United States rather than subscribe to the Revolution and the Declaration of Independence. They had left rich holdings for pittances in New Brunswick—pittances yes, but held under the Crown. This, too, would remain central to Cecil Bennett all his life.

When elections came, the divisions among New Brunswickers swept the province like the tides of Fundy. A young lad without a penny in his pocket could get hours of free entertainment from the shoutings of the stump-orators. If he was lucky, a gifted giant like William Pugsley, a former provincial premier who could beguile an audience for hours, might descend from Saint John. Besides the orations and the antics of the crowd, there were the bonfires and torchlight parades of victory, and the burning in effigy of those who had gone down in defeat. For the young Bennett, all these moments must have joined as one when the greatest of them all, Sir Wilfrid Laurier, came down to stump the hustings, fighting poll by poll for one large issue—reciprocity—the question of trade and how much of it Canada should have with the United States.

When Laurier came, Cecil Bennett heard him. By all accounts, the prime minister gave a great performance. The ten-year-old boy watched him leave and then joined the crowd around the bonfire. They were burning Sir Wilfrid in effigy, and as the flames curled around the parody of Laurier's face, grade-schooler Cecil Bennett made a vow to become as brave, as intransigent and as principled as the man he had heard on that day.

In 1911, WHEN I WAS ten years old, there was a federal election on reciprocity. Looking back, I think Laurier was right; we should have had reciprocity with the United States. But we were against it then, because our people were Imperial Loyalists; we were Conservatives.

I got enthused about the campaign and I'd hitch a ride to any political meeting anywhere, no matter which party was holding it. I was greatly influenced by many different political speakers, both provincially in New Brunswick and nationally. I was struck by the fact that because they had to toe the party line, some of them advocated policies they didn't really believe in. I enquired why they had this allegiance to party. Why?

Well, suppose you're a lawyer: you've got to obey the party line if you want to become a judge, or go to the Senate. If you're going into the contracting business, you've got to obey the party to get the contracts. And I can mention a dozen other things. I noticed all that as a very small boy.

I saw so many politicians collapse for different reasons, mostly from liquor. I was too poor to smoke or drink, and I was tinged with what some might call a strong religious belief. So I didn't do it. I found it easier not to smoke or drink. If you smoke, you have to make a decision every day how many times you're going to have another cigarette. If you make one decision that you're not going to smoke at all, that's the easy way to do it. If you make a rule that you're not going to drink, you only make the decision once. If somebody offers you a drink, you say, "Yes thanks, ginger ale or Ovaltine."

Other politicians collapsed because they owed various debts to various groups; to labour, management—any group. In the end, they ruined their careers because they weren't free to make the decisions they ought to have made at the time.

I could see patronage everywhere. It is the cancer in the democratic parliamentary system of government. But I always said, "That's not for me, that's *not* for me."

These ideas come to you even when you're young. Your mind is clear then, clearer than at any other time in your life. And the things that happen then will influence your whole life. When I was a young kid, I made a commitment to myself that politics would be my career.

After Cecil Bennett completed grade school in Hampton, he dug in his heels and refused to go on to high school. There were loud arguments in the family and quiet determined moves by his mother, but young Cecil held out; he wanted practical experience, not more theoretical stuff shoved at him in a classroom. He wanted to get out into the world and make his mark.

Finally, a truce was arranged. His brother, Russell, took him down to Saint John and found him part-time employment with the hardware merchants, Robertson, Foster and Smith. In return, Cecil promised he would finish high school.

With a war going on in Europe, the hardware business boomed; supplies were needed for wagons and tents and other equipment the army was using up at a rapid rate. Cecil had to learn fast, but he had old Foster to teach him. Cecil's employer was the brother of Walter Foster, who became premier of New Brunswick in 1917. By paying Cecil only part of his salary, and keeping back the rest until the lad had shown he could handle the amount he had been paid, Foster combined old-fashioned business practices with political astuteness. He also lectured the boy on Liberal politics, for the Fosters had been stalwarts in Laurier's party since Confederation.

The war in Europe ground on. After three years of inept generalship and wholesale slaughter, a few rays of tactical sunshine broke through the mists surrounding the Allied High Command. It began to realize that there might be other uses for the flying machines that had been restricted to such mundane roles as spotting enemy artillery or observing troop movements. An Australian, General John Monash, had successfully employed aircraft to strafe German positions in his attack on Hamel in August 1918. By co-ordinating tank and aircraft movements to stun and stupefy the enemy, he had taken all his objectives in a single day, sustaining only light casualties. Now the Allied High Command made plans to launch a grand fall offensive using full-scale air power.

One obstacle stood in the way of such a plan. There weren't enough pilots to carry it out. The year 1917 had seen a slaughter in the air proportionate to the killings on the Somme and at Passchendaele. The Germans had always enjoyed a slight edge in the quality of their machines. Now they had evolved a new and far more murderous way of air-fighting. Gangs of airplanes roamed the sky seeking outnumbered and preferably under-powered foes. Their strategy was to kill the pilot rather than shoot down his machine.

Experienced Allied flyers protected themselves by staying in close formation. But there were few with expertise and many novices. Often a boy would be sent up after no more than a few hours flying solo over the peaceful fields of Kent. In the skies over France he faced an aerial circus led by such aces as Baron Manfred von Richthofen. Young British pilots' lives in the air were short, and few ever saw the enemy who shot them down.

The solution was to upgrade the quality of pilot training. But time was running out and politicians were clamouring for an Allied victory. The generals persuaded the British government to lower the age limit for enlistment in the Royal Flying Corps. When it was dropped in Britain from eighteen to seventeen and a half, the governments in the Dominions, including Canada's, quickly followed suit.

All this directly affected young Cecil Bennett, who had heard about the romantic life of a pilot—the knight of the skies, jousting in single combat with the evil Hun. Cecil wanted to get into war service in the Royal Flying Corps, or the Royal Air Force, as it had just been renamed. The air war had created some real heroes; Roy Brown, "Wop" May and others had become household words in Canada. There were reports of May flying his first mission when he was attacked by von Richthofen; of Brown swooping down on the Red Baron's tail and sending his craft spinning to the ground, where it burst into flames. Then there was the legendary Billy Bishop, who may not have fought like a gentleman—after all, he was still alive—but the journalists made him sound like one. What boy could resist the pull of such magnetic personalities, such derring-do, such bravery? When the age was lowered, Cecil Bennett was among the first to rush to the door of the recruiting office.

The recruiters were only too happy to sign him up. They read him the King's Regulations, and from that moment on he was bound by military law; he had become a soldier in the Canadian Army of King George V. However, that was as far as it went. Hundreds of lads had to be processed, but uniforms were available for barely a dozen of them. In the fourth year of the Great War, men had to wait until they reached their training camps before being given a uniform; even those who were about to join the heroic aces in the air over France were no exception. Cecil Bennett was among those who were told to go back to school or work and wait for the call.

W. A. C. Bennett had to wait his turn. When the Germans mobilized their shock troops to counter the Allied build-up, authorities in Canada panicked. It was ground troops that were in demand, and once again, sending young airmen overseas had to be laid aside. But when the British and the French struck at the German-held Marne crossings, optimism returned.

In a mood charged with urgency, the Allies again planned a counter-stroke. To the people in Canada it looked as if this attack might be the last one of the war. Once more Ottawa sent out a call for pilots, and once more the orders had to be counter-manded—this time because an epidemic had broken out and was sweeping the country. They called it the Spanish Flu, which spared the old but struck down the young. Having begun its rampage in the East in August, the disease spread into Ontario. Camp Borden, where Cecil was to have received his training, had to be closed. By September, the flu had reached Manitoba; by October, Alberta. The death toll began to drop only as winter approached, and on November 11, 1918 the war in Europe was over. The generals of the opposing armies met in the Forest of Compiègne to sign an armistice, and out in Saint John, New Brunswick young Cecil Bennett was still waiting to get into a uniform.

MY FATHER WAS OVERSEAS with the Canadian Army, but I had promised my mother that I wouldn't try to enlist until I was of legal age and would stay in school until then. But in the spring of 1918 they were short of airmen, and the Canadian Government, in its wisdom or lack thereof, reduced the enlistment age to seventeen and a half. On the day I turned seventeen and a half, I enlisted in the Royal Air Force. I was supposed to go to Camp Borden but although I was ready to go I never got there because there was disease in the camp.

Canadian National Telegraph and Canadian Pacific Telegraph weren't connected as they are today. So, I'd get one telegram from Ottawa via Canadian National telling me to go, and five minutes later another one via Canadian Pacific saying I should stay. I'd try to find out which one had been sent first but no one knew; there was so much red tape. When the war ended I'd never even put on a uniform.

As you could have your discharge wherever you wanted to have it, I studied the map of Canada well. I looked at the Northwest Territories, then back at little New Brunswick. When I saw Alberta and Edmonton, I said to myself that's where I want to get my discharge. So I travelled across Canada, at a cost of about one cent a mile, and saw a lot of great country that was practically empty of people and needing development.

~ 2~

Opportunity
to Buy

Fifty thousand people were living in Edmonton when Cecil
Bennett arrived. There was little industry, but all around were
mixed farms, cattle ranches and wheat fields. Especially wheat—
Manitoba Hard, that rich, glutinous strain that was making the
Prairies famous the world over. All the produce of the region—
cattle, skins, everything—poured through the funnel of
Edmonton.

The city was a wide-open, barren sort of place, especially
to someone used to the verdant slopes of the Kennebacasis River.
Along Jasper Avenue, a few two- and three-storey brick buildings stood in clumps, marking the corners of still-to-be-built
side streets. In between were stores with false fronts separated by
weed-infested vacant lots.

One block, and sometimes even less, off Jasper Avenue,
paving stopped and gravel became the road surface for a short
distance, followed by mud or hard, dry dust. Streetcars lurched
along the city's main streets, then lumbered slowly through
stretches of forest to reach the next settled area. Although the
tents that had earlier fringed the outskirts of the city were now
gone, as were the saloons and mobile real estate offices, the aura
of frontier clung, with a vision of tumbleweed and the sour
smell of rotgut whiskey.

Still, Edmonton was fast climbing upward toward respect-
ability and the problems of a modern metropolis. In the years
before the Great War, the city had thrived, 1912 having been its
all-time boom year. New subdivisions had been spawned, with
streetcar lines marching out to them. Edmonton had swallowed
the nearby town of Strathcona, reaching out to Calder and

beyond. As the Hudson's Bay Company sold off the remnants of its enormous domains, new land reserves were opened up. So vast was the business that it spilled out into the streets, with curbstone brokers operating around the railroad stations. The strangers who got off the trains were offered lots these brokers had bought on one-dollar options. Money flowed from block-busting and illegal land hoardings, and much of it ended up in the pockets of the city's aldermen. It was a wonderful time to make a lot of money!

In that same year, the Canadian Northern Railway finished its link to Alberta's north, replacing an old wagon trail. Then came the opening of the High Level Bridge, 2,555 feet of steel on piers 100 feet high, carrying railway tracks, a double street-car track, a roadway and dual sidewalks across the Saskatchewan River. This structure and the illuminated sign on Bob Mc-Donald's hotel, which showed a man pouring a glass of beer and then drinking it, were regarded as the great marvels of the boom period.

But by the time W. A. C. Bennett arrived in Edmonton, oil fever had replaced land speculation. Calgary had brought in the Dingman oil well. Share prices jumped from $12.50 to $200 overnight and forty new oil companies hit the market in one week. The money fled from Edmonton to the upstart town in the south.

When young Bennett stepped off the train, the Canadian Northern railway station was not even as old as he was. The line was in deep financial trouble, and even the Canadian Pacific Railway, the second railway in town, was discovering that there were neither enough people nor enough goods available to run a system across the nation profitably. By 1919, both lines were racked by troubles and the Canadian Northern was about to declare bankruptcy.

The Edmonton streets Cecil Bennett walked along were a liability to the city fathers. The tax rolls had been readjusted. Property that had been bought on margin during the boom now had to be confiscated by the city, because the people who had bought could not pay the taxes.

But young Bennett was restless and eager to get on. Other young men had arrived: "Punch" Dickens, George Gorman, "Wop" May, Roy Brown and Jimmy Bell. They had been war pilots and, like Cecil Bennett, began to look beyond the city's limits, past the vast and rich farmlands, beyond the thinly settled pastures to the remote and resource-rich North. "Wop"

May founded May Airplanes Ltd. and flew newspapers and passengers to the North. George Gorman was hired to fly Imperial Oil's rented planes to the new oil fields at Fort Norman.

Cecil Bennett chose to stick with the hardware business. His Saint John apprenticeship served him well in a city that had to supply the needs of thousands of farmers—bridles and snaffles for their horses, bolts and studs for their wagons, nails and fittings for their barns. They came to the men who sold the stuff.

WHEN I ARRIVED in Edmonton, I got a job with the Marshall Wells Company, which at that time was the world's largest hardware wholesaler.

Soon I became assistant sales manager and had to set up programs for all the salesmen and department managers. Every salesman got a quota not only for a twelve-month period but for each month as well. The figures weren't pulled out of a hat, but were based on past experience and on percentages of what ought to be done in a twelve-month period.

There were sixteen departments at Marshall Wells. Each month I allocated a percentage to each department. At the end of every month I handed a statement to each salesman so that he would know exactly how much he'd earned that month and what kind of bonus he'd receive at the end of the year. That's how you have to handle salesmen—keep them informed. Our sales were enormous and our salesmen received enormous bonuses.

In Edmonton, our sales increased faster than at any of the other Marshall Wells branches. As tangible proof of our efforts, we won cups; there was the President's Cup and others, which are still on display in the Edmonton store even though Marshall Wells is now owned by different people.

But I wanted more; I wanted to be on my own and didn't think my career should be with a big company. So I looked for an opportunity to buy a hardware business.

In February 1927, Mr. Joe Renaud and I opened a hardware store in Westlock, Alberta. Joe was a brilliant young

French Canadian with a good head on his shoulders. He had been a school teacher and, like me, he was a good family man; but in everything else—in religion and in language, we were opposites. Although he and his brother-in-law fought all the time, he and I never had a verbal battle, or any other battle for that matter, during the three years we were business partners. I like the French people.

Our business prospered right through 1927 and 1928. Renaud and I had based it on sound business principles. We stuck to them and were prepared to work hard.

One day a pleasant chap came into the store to buy a whole lot of merchandise. He paid me by cheque and then said, "Now, Mr. Bennett, I want you to take me back to the hotel and we'll have a few drinks together, to celebrate."

I tried to get out of it as nicely as I could, but he kept insisting, and in the end I had to tell him that it was against my principles to drink.

"Well," he said, "if you can't drink with me, you can't do business with me."

I said, "I'm sorry, exceedingly sorry." The sale went back. It was too bad that my partner had not been in the store at the time, because he drank and he smoked too.

Two or three weeks went by, when this same person returned to the store and placed an order with me. When he was about to leave, I asked him, "What did you come back for?"

"Well," he replied, "I have sent four people in here, because I wanted to see if by any chance you'd take a drink with them. But you didn't. If you had, I would never have come back."

I believe that if you have a rule, you must keep it. Mind you, I never objected to anyone else taking a drink; that was their business. But I would tell them, "Thanks, but I make my decisions, and you can make yours."

I had a strong religious background, first in New Brunswick and then in Alberta. I worked in boys' church movements, and taught Sunday School in Edmonton to young Chinese immigrants and helped them with their school work. I was greatly interested in teaching moral value, and, at one time, I had thought of becoming a minister.

That's where my wife and I first met, at a meeting between her church and mine. Annie Elizabeth May Richards was from Wellington in British Columbia and had come to Edmonton to teach school. I thought she'd make a great wife and a great mother, and be a great citizen. Also, she was interested in all the things I was interested in. I think it is important to marry somebody who shares your interests and has the same basic beliefs, the same basic hopes.

May's girlfriends tried to talk with her about me and tell her, "Don't marry that Cecil Bennett, he's not going to last very long." But apparently she could see in me something these other women couldn't see. We got married on July 11, 1927, and her good cooking did a lot for me to build me up.

We first rented a house instead of buying one because I wanted to pour every dollar back into the business. Then we began to raise a family. Our daughter Anita was born first. Russell J. came next. Bill was born later in Kelowna. When the 1920s came to an end, I found myself in business with a growing family.

My father-in-law was an inspector of mines for the government of Alberta. He and I discussed politics a lot when he was at our house, a thing he couldn't do outside because he was a civil servant. My wife might say, "Too bad you didn't tell me before we married that you wanted to go into politics," but her father and I talked about it more than about anything else.

About that time I made my decision; by taking up a career in politics rather than in the church, I felt I could make a greater contribution. People can develop talents, but they must also be born with at least one or two of them. Whether you become a sculptor or a painter, a poet or a mechanic, you are born with the talents you later develop. I was adept in mathematics and finance, and I thought I could make a special contribution to the financial structure of government.

~ 3 ~

The Ideal Climate

1921 had brought lingering recession and new strains to Edmonton's slowly recovering economy, but no one panicked. The men who had returned from the war were steadier than the speculators and profiteers who had held sway in the city earlier. Farmers still bought cars, their wives ordered goods from the Marshall Wells catalogue, and no one packed his bags to leave the city.

Bennett the optimist sided with the folk who said that any young man willing to work hard could amount to something. He proved that in five years one can rise from pushing a hand cart in the stock room to managing Marshall Wells' northern Alberta district.

He must have thanked whatever luck rode with him from New Brunswick that he had not joined his parents, who had gone to homestead in the Peace River Country of British Columbia. He might have wondered why fate had brought him to a city which was as raw and as new as himself. But the canniness that had parlayed a period of non-service in the Air Force into a trip across a continent had not deserted him. His sense of looking to see what was past the next corner was telling him to set his sights beyond Westlock and Edmonton.

IN 1928, I NOTICED that wheat, the main product of the Prairies, did not sell. The Canadian wheat pools were fighting for markets and held back the grain they couldn't sell, trying to set a world price. Later it was proved that this cannot be done by one country alone.

Then came the 1929 crash. I had studied the stock market

and knew what made prices rise and fall, and what the effects of these fluctuations were. I also saw that the banks had only given credit to those companies with which they were closely connected. By their actions they had closed every other business.

Our hardware store in Westlock was in fairly good shape, but the wheat didn't sell, and the world stock markets had collapsed. That was a warning that a storm was brewing and a depression was on its way. A one-crop country was no place to be during a depression. So I decided to sell my share in the Westlock business and move. The negotiations dragged on and on and the deal didn't go through until the spring of 1930. I sold my interest at one hundred cents on the wholesale dollar, 100 percent of the wholesalers' merchandise cost price.

We left Westlock in June 1930 for Victoria, where my wife had a maiden aunt, Elizabeth Russell, who'd been staying with us in Alberta. She opened up her house.

I knew of Kelowna, in British Columbia's Okanagan Valley. They had irrigation there, so they could be sure of a beautiful crop and lots of food. A place with lots of sun and lots of water. You can talk about all the resources in the world, about oil and natural gas, but the most important is fresh water. It's more valuable than all the other resources put together; that's the reason why we should be storing more water everywhere we can, where it's not interfering with the fish.

Kelowna also had the ideal climate in which to raise a family. The summer was awfully hot that year and we decided that my wife and the children should stay in Victoria for awhile and I would drive to Kelowna alone. It was a terrible trip; the highways were in such bad condition that I had to go via the United States.

I acquired a business in Kelowna from a chap who was scared of the Depression and wanted out. I bought it at a 32 percent discount of his wholesale cost price. That gave my store a leeway, a good margin to begin with. We had difficult times in Kelowna during the Depression, but not as difficult as they were in the Prairies or elsewhere in Canada.

In some ways, the Depression did not appear to touch Cecil Bennett at all. While other men had been scarred and made cautious by the experience, he seemed as ebullient as ever. His hardware store, as U.S. president Calvin Coolidge might have put it, "was in the business of making business."

Politically, he also held his ground. The winds that blew images of change out of the dust of a collapsing system passed him by. He knew about the Ku Klux Klan, who had burnt a cross in Alberta, and he also was aware that hooded riders were enjoying some support in the Okanagan. In the twenties, politicians there had won votes by raising the spectre of the "Oriental menace," frightening white farmers with the prospect that a flood of "the brown-skinned sons of Nippon" and the "insidious Chinee" would take away their land. In fact, the so-called "Orientals" owned only 125 acres of the hundreds of thousands in the valley.

All across Canada, new movements arose to challenge the beaten concepts of the old. In Quebec, Adrien Arcand raised a swastika banner with a hooked cross surrounded by bold maple leaves surmounted by a rather rat-like beaver. Although the flag lacked aesthetics, it drew the crowds, and soon the beaver was bobbing above a forest of outstretched fascist arms.

The cycle of debt and drought ground down the farmers. They brought out their horses to plough the fields; their new tractors were left to rust in the sheds. The shiny cars and sturdy trucks acquired during the good times sat idle. There was no money to buy fuel. But the farmers found their buggies and buckboards had rotted through neglect. They attached tongues and cross-trees to their useless cars, hitched them to the horses and rode around in them. These "Bennett Buggies," named after Prime Minister R. B. Bennett, carried them past the banks they owed money to, past the fields where their dead cattle lay on parched and cracked ground, past the Russian thistles growing abundantly—the only plants that could flourish in Prairie drought conditions.

In 1932, the discontented and dispossessed met in Calgary to form a new party—the Co-operative Commonwealth Federation. A year later they issued their Regina Manifesto, which had some of William Blake's fiery tongues of prophecy in it. They said that their swords would not sleep in their hands until capitalism had been put to rest and a Co-operative Commonwealth was founded in Canada's dry, unsettled land.

Oh, the arrows of desire were flying everywhere, hitting people in the most unlikely places. In 1935, R. B. Bennett let the iron heels of his boots stray from the centre to the left. Fighting an election with a divided cabinet, he ran on a platform of "radical social reform." He offered unemployment insurance, minimum wages, limitations of work hours and a standard of treatment for employees.

This platform shocked Cecil Bennett and the other devoted Conservative cadres. To them, it was socialism with a vengeance.

R. B. Bennett lost the election and the Supreme Court of Canada ruled that his suggested reforms were not within the constitutional powers of the federal government. The loyal Conservatives heaved a sigh of relief, even though "that man," Mackenzie King, was now in power.

But their relief was short-lived, as the new prime minister soon began looking for ways to broaden the federal government's mandate in the welfare field. It was an area that cried out for definition. Municipalities were already dependent on federal and provincial handouts. In Newfoundland, families received six cents a head for their daily food—in Ontario, those on relief had to surrender driver's licenses or license plates to assure officials that the money was not being used for joyriding.

But to Cecil Bennett and other Conservatives, King's relief programs smacked of "The New Deal" all over again. In the United States, Franklin D. Roosevelt had campaigned on a platform that had promised cuts in government spending, reductions in taxes and incentives to get private industries moving, promises tinged with a most Republican hue. But once in office, F. D. R.'s administration had spawned a medley of welfare agencies and projects, even causing some of his old supporters to mutter darkly about "Moscow on the Potomac" and a Red President in the White House.

Cecil Bennett's reaction to such policies makes sense from today's vantage point. As G. K. Chesterton observed:

The term "reactionary" is generally used as a term of offence, just as the term "progressive" is used as a term of praise; but only once in a hundred times is either of them used so as to convey any meaning of truth. . . . Progress happens . . . whenever men can endure one tendency for a long time. And reaction happens whenever some particular man can endure it no longer . . . the progressive is always a conservative; he conserves the direction of progress. A reactionary is always a rebel.

Quoted from "Carlyle's 'Past and Present'—An Introduction." In *Selected Modern English Essays*, Sir Humphrey Milford. Oxford University Press, 1925.

Bennett believed this; it was the final glaze to his political clay. He felt that measures such as Roosevelt was applying and Mackenzie King was seeking to effect might help in the short term; but taken in the longer perspective, they could only lead to the massive interventionist and centralized state promised by the socialists. To W. A. C. Bennett, the old parties were simply capitulating to the call for collective action. The pattern of excessive spending and heavy taxation would turn into the habit of deficit financing, resulting in spiralling inflation. A far worse collapse than the previous one lurked at the end of that road. In 1935, Canadians might be riding to their doom in Bennett Buggies, but somewhere in the future they would face a greater catastrophe, seated in armchairs provided by the government. In that respect, Cecil Bennett was more progressive in Chesterton's sense of the word than the bureaucrats who began to flock into Ottawa.

But there was an alternative to Cecil Bennett's gloomy assumptions. The year in which Prime Minister R. B. Bennett hoisted his own brand of the "Red Flag" also saw a Calgary high-school teacher and lay preacher lead a new party to victory in Alberta, fighting the election on policies directly opposed to prevailing trends.

William Aberhart, inflamed by the sight of his best students graduating to a future that offered nothing more than enforced idleness, could see that the pattern of things had to be changed. *He* was a true reactionary. Through his sermons and letters to the newspapers, he began to flog the system, but other than moral outrage, he had nothing to offer in its place. Then, in 1934, he discovered Social Credit. Charles Scarborough, a friend living in Edmonton, had introduced him to the writings of Clifford Hugh Douglas, a British major who extolled the primacy of the individual, making the consumer the only object of production. Douglas preached against bankers and financiers who artificially restricted credit for their own ends. In 1935, Aberhart was able to battle his monsters armed with a new and viable political theory.

Albertans had suffered through four years of drought and dust, clad in gunny sacks. They were ready to hit out at anything and anyone. William Aberhart blazed a trail of oratory through the desolate farmlands and destitute towns of the province; his campaign combined an almost mystical fervour with the cunning trickery of a medicine show. In some places, he would appear on the speakers' platform dressed in rags. As he tore off each worn-out piece of clothing, he would identify it with a part of the old economic system. Gradually, from beneath the rags, would emerge a brand-new suit, a suit, he would tell his audience, that personified Social Credit and that could only be seen when all the dregs of the old order had been thrown into the sewers where they belonged.

Aberhart's impact was baffling to outsiders. Stephen Leacock described the phenomenon as "certain profundities of British fog, impossible for most people to understand, which in sunny Alberta, by force of prayer, turned into Alberta Social Credit." But Leacock's Mariposa had no drought. Alberta did. To Albertans, Social Credit was like a pillar of fire leading a Chosen People.

Cecil Bennett scoffed at Aberhart's histrionics, condemning his economic theories as nothing more than a veneer to give empty-headed nonsense a shimmer of profundity. "Certainly," he said, "anyone would grab at an offer of $25 a month handed out as a basic dividend; but where is that money coming from?" The promise of a new currency based on public credit in the province was sure to shatter against the Canadian constitution which reserved to the federal government the right to print money.

It is hard to imagine now why people in Alberta treated Social Credit as if it were the Second Coming. Men cheerfully lined up to receive their basic dividend so that their wives could pick the best from the mail order catalogues. Some employees even quit their old jobs, convinced that a better one was just around the corner.

But Aberhart soon found out that the provincial debt was too great to allow his theories to be carried out fully, just yet. He was forced to go on the radio to lament that he felt like the young woman, who, in the pangs of childbirth, had cried out, "If this is what marriage is like, you can tell the young man the engagement is off."

Although W. A. C. Bennett's skepticism about Social Credit seemed justified, William Aberhart's political know-how did influence him later. The way he had organized and conducted his campaign had impressed Bennett. Aberhart did not personally supervise the creation of small study groups, sixteen hundred of them at their peak, that met in school houses, town halls and church basements. But when he arrived to deliver his speech, there was no need to persuade his listeners; he just preached to the converted. Another thing that appealed to Bennett was Aberhart's capacity for reason before action. He had initially gone to all three provincial parties—the Liberals, the Conservatives and the United Farmers—asking them to make Social Credit a plank in their platforms. They had met his proposals with either sneers or silence. Only then had he thrown himself wholeheartedly into the task of forming a new party. Once it was created and the tide had turned in its favour, he begged off running for a place in the provincial sun. What he wanted, he said, was to remain at the heart of the party and be its inspiration and drive. Yet a seat was found in the Okotoks–High River riding and the premiership was apparently "forced upon him."

Was this a commendable modesty on the part of a man who was a teacher at heart, or was it subtle and cunning strategy? Not even Aberhart's closest associates knew for sure. But one thing was certain: the tactics by which he had created and controlled the upheaval that *was* Alberta Social Credit had not been lost on William A. Cecil Bennett. He made several arduous journeys to Alberta and Saskatchewan to gather unemployed people and bring them to the Okanagan to farm. During these trips, he discovered a surprisingly high energy in himself, an ebullience that never faltered despite evidence of defeat all around him. He also drove himself hard in his business to create an economic base that would allow him to enter politics unhampered by financial pressures.

I WAS WORKING hard in my new store from early morning until late at night. Our maiden aunt from Victoria then came to Kelowna with my wife and our two children. Remember, it was depression time and hundreds of people would stop by our home asking for a meal. Some were tramps, others were looking for work, and many left marks to let those that followed know that our house was a good place to stop and ask for food.

Our fuel was wood at that time, and I had to chop the wood. So I said to my wife and her aunt, "From now on, any person that comes in and asks for a meal, I would like you to ask him to go out and chop a little wood while you get the kettle on." They thought that was awfully cruel.

I said, "No, that's not the whole story. Those that go out the gate and don't pick up the axe, don't need it anyway. But those that pick up the axe, don't let them do it a second time. Stop them, and bring them in. By now you've let them separate themselves."

It worked wonderfully well. That was a tough period for the genuine people; but for the real tramp it was the greatest time in history, because everybody wanted to help him. It brought the best out of people.

In Kelowna the spirit was good. So many decent people needed help. The feeling, not only in our church but in all of town, was, "How can we help those who have suffered from the drought on the Prairies?"

I had visited Regina; not only had I seen the dust blowing, but when I walked down the street, grasshoppers were jumping all over my coat. I felt we had to do something to help people.

I became vice-president of the Kelowna Board of Trade, the Chamber of Commerce. The farmers had donated apples to the drought areas of Saskatchewan, and we encouraged the railways to haul them in bulk. We had a surplus of good apples and it was hard to sell them anyway. There was an abundance of tomatoes, which cost very little. We stocked canning machines in our store and also supplied cans—"two-and-a-halfs" they called them—to preserve the thousands and thousands of pounds of tomatoes. We shipped carloads full of unlabelled cans in among the apples.

The people in the drought area of Saskatchewan welcomed this food from Kelowna. They said, "Gee, that must be the place to be." So they left Saskatchewan and came to us by the hundreds and hundreds. They were willing to work hard and today those former Prairie people and their descendants are our best citizens.

~ 4 ~

Principles
and Policies

In Kelowna the Bennetts quickly became involved in church
and Red Cross activities. Cecil joined the Gyros, a service club
similar to the Lions or Rotarians, and some of these community
involvements soon paid off. He was invited to political gather-
ings, including one in nearby Summerland at which he sat on
the platform with Grote Stirling, the incumbent Tory member.
With him was H. A. Truswell, the "kingmaker" in the
Okanagan Valley, and he and Bennett were soon talking to
each other. Theirs was to be a long-lasting and well-chosen
alliance.

The Conservative Party in British Columbia has a varied
history. Before 1903, its members had formed loose associations
with others that sometimes united them but more often were
divisive. In 1903, the provincial parties reorganized along
federal lines, grouping themselves into Liberals and Conservatives—a nominal distinction, since a study of party platforms,
resolutions by local and provincial associations, Speeches from
the Throne and debates in the legislature reveals not one whit
of difference between them.

Their policies, however, seemed radical compared to those
practised on the other side of the Rockies. Both parties favoured
some government involvement in labour disputes and some
government participation in railways, telephone systems and
public utilities. Both parties would have liked to supply aid to
those settling the land, provide health insurance, old age and
mother's pensions, and abolish property taxes by extending
income taxes. These were radical notions in the early years of
this century. They were promoted by two equally powerful
groups, together exerting democratic pressure of a kind that

elsewhere in the country had been achieved only through pro-
tests or threats of revolt. These two groups were the farmers and
the industrial workers.

British Columbia Conservatives were the first to form a
government along these lines, and immediately they exhibited
a talent for internal slaughter that echoed the bloody tribal
fights of the earlier West Coast Indians. Richard McBride (later
Sir Richard) became their official leader in 1904, and within
weeks he was feuding with no less a notable Tory than Sir
Charles Tupper, former leader of the Dominion Conservatives.
Neither man would admit the reason for their feuding, but
gossip had it that someone's nose had been put out of joint over
an insufficient reward for outstanding party service. After all,
patronage was the axe that severed unity just as often as it was
the dynamo that ran the party machine. McBride hung on until
1916, gratefully relinquishing his post to receive a British
knighthood. His successor, W. J. Bowser, had no better luck
with Sir Charles; in fact, during the 1916 election Tupper toured
the province urging voters to defeat every provincial Conservative who supported Bowser. Needless to say, the Conservatives
were thrashed by the Liberals under Harlan Brewster.

The Liberals ruled in Victoria from the thirteenth to the
fifteenth provincial parliament. Meanwhile the Conservatives
ran in all directions at the same time—Imperial Conservatives,
McBride Conservatives, Independent Conservatives and Unionists,
each group throwing as much mud at its rival factions as it
could gather, while the Young Conservatives, who appeared to
have the covert backing of Tupper, happily destroyed the repu-
tations of all the others.

In 1918, John Oliver, a passionate opponent of patronage,
became Liberal premier. He created a civil service commission
to deal with patronage, hoping that the favours of government
would be handed out on merit alone. His actions threatened to
lead the Liberals into as great a state of disarray as the
Conservatives. Traditionally, British Columbia office holders
and the leading men in local and provincial associations had
met to decide who would be rewarded and who could be safely
passed over in the current round of debt-paying. Now the chiefs
themselves had been passed over. In 1922, John Oliver, faced by
the provincial leadership convention, had to capitulate. "We in
the innocence of our hearts," he said, "have passed over to a
commission patronage rights that should have been exercised
by the members of the government and the representatives of

the people. The results are not satisfactory." His audience beamed. At last power was back in the hands of the party.

In 1928, Dr. Simon Fraser Tolmie swept into power with a reinvigorated Conservative party, having captured thirty-five out of the forty-seven seats in the provincial legislature. But Tolmie had a genius for miscalculation. There had been rumblings from those voters who traditionally supported third parties like the small-potatoes People's Party. It displaced the Provincial Party, which in turn had taken over from the Farmer's Party. None of these groups had anything more inspiring to offer than a general call to turn out John Oliver and keep out W. J. Bowser. Their place was taken by a freshly organized Labour Party that carried within it the seeds of the future provincial CCF. As Tolmie acceded to power, Labour's voice was the loudest, clamouring for change and challenging the system he represented. With the healthy majority he commanded, Tolmie had a golden moment in which to make the beleaguered system work. Instead, he created three more portfolios in his cabinet to show his gratitude to those from whom he had received favours earlier. Patronage was back, and it was all downhill from there.

By the spring of 1931, Tolmie's government was in chaos. The hammer that would smash his administration appeared one morning on the steps of the legislative building. A deputation from twenty-two organizations had come to ask the premier to appoint a committee to investigate the whole field of government finances. Tolmie had to listen, for they represented the Vancouver Board of Trade, the Canadian Manufacturers' Association, the Victoria Chamber of Commerce, the Retail Merchants' Association, five Vancouver service clubs—in short, most of the money in the province.

He had to give in. In fact, he went even further. He allowed them to select eight names from which he would choose five to sit on the committee. It is doubtful if, since then, any politician has ever strangled himself in public so completely as Tolmie did on that spring day. The Kidd Committee, as it was called, brought in its deliberations in the spring of 1932. Since increased taxation was an impossibility, they recommended that $6 million be lopped off a provincial budget which totalled a mere $25 million. They proposed to make these cuts by carving one-third out of the education budget: 25 percent of all teachers in the province would be dismissed; the university would be closed and the salaries of all remaining teachers cut by 25 percent. That much Tolmie might have swallowed, but what stuck in his gullet was the recommendation that the seats in the legislature be reduced to twenty-eight and that the number of cabinet members be cut from eleven to six. There was also a damaging section in the report which attacked the party system, accusing it of creating difficulties through excessive expenditures. "Political life," it went on to say, "had largely become a struggle between one party to retain and the other to recapture the benefits of office."

By the time the Kidd Report was published, Tolmie had lost his grip. He reluctantly offered Bowser and Pattullo, the Liberal leader, posts in a new Unionist government if they would support him. Rejected by both, he tried a new approach, begging the executive of the provincial party association to stay out of the forthcoming election. Conservatives would be free to campaign under whatever title they wished—Union Conservative, Independent, Non-Partisan—a whole bagful of names. By this move, Tolmie hoped to gather the many-coloured coats of the victorious candidates and transform them into the one hue of Conservatism which he intended to lead in the House. But his plan was thwarted by the Bowserites, who formed what they called a "citizenship movement;" this would be non-partisan, in accordance with the lines laid down in the Kidd Report. Rather than risk losing control to Bowser, Tolmie took the sad remnants of his cabinet to the lieutenant-governor and asked him to dissolve the government.

An unrepentant Bowserite wrote to the *Victoria Daily Times*, "For the last four or five years a number of us have been trying to build up a political movement behind W. J. Bowser that would give Conservatives an opportunity to vote for men of their own party and principles without having to be associated with the incompetent Tolmie crowd." That letter was written in 1933, the year T. D. Pattullo's Liberals cruised into the legislature with thirty-four seats, the CCF coming in with seven to form the official opposition. One of Tolmie's men staggered in and the Bowserites elected two. Tom Uphill sat as the Labour Party member, and two independents stood for matters they kept to themselves.

Taking into account the events that flowed from 1931, it did not seem a good time for Cecil Bennett to sit on that Conservative platform that day in Summerland. But like many apparent contradictions in his life, it was one of the best times for him to join the Conservative Party. The Bowser feud was smouldering to an end, and long, lean years stretched ahead. The Conservatives would need new blood.

In 1933, Cecil Bennett had the opportunity to watch T. D. Pattullo, the province's first modern political leader, grasp the Liberal premiership. As minister in charge of the Lands Department, Pattullo had been one of the quiet men in the rowdy cabinets of earlier Liberal governments, looking after his constituents, keeping abuses of land laws within reasonable bounds and maintaining a moderate approach to problems that cried out for radical solutions. Had the Liberals remained in power, his moderation might have ossified; but the onset of the Depression corresponded to Pattullo's own years out of power, and in place of action he had to resort to meditation about how the state could play a creative role in restoring a ravaged economy. He spurned the socialists, whose notions of equality outraged his sense of the individual's aspirations. At the same time, he rejected letting the power of private business go unchecked. Having watched Tolmie in somnolent action, Pattullo had determined that the day could not be far off when he would lead the Liberals and the province with a type of government they had not seen before.

But the new premier's attempts at reform did not sit well in places like the Okanagan Valley. At Summerland, Peachland, Westbank and right up to Kelowna, the farmers felt that Pattullo was leading the province into the arms of the Bolsheviks. Finance Minister John Hart's budget exempted low wage earners from a special 1 percent tax. A new Minimum Wage Act was passed and the government voted $3 million for unemployment relief. If that was not enough to set Tory tongues wagging, Bill 36 provided broad powers to the cabinet during specified periods of time, allowing it to sell and dispose of natural resources, borrow and lend money and suspend property and civil rights. Known as the Special Powers Act, it turned the invective from comparisons with Lenin's and Stalin's policies to remarks about the new Mussolinis and Hitlers now sitting in Victoria, B.C.

The flurry of bills was not enough to stem the tide of the onrushing Depression; Pattullo was forced to go to Ottawa to beg for money. Prime Minister R. B. Bennett may not have liked Pattullo's legislation, but he could not help but admire the way in which the man moved in on areas of federal authority. For a start, he demanded that all income tax powers be transferred to British Columbia. He then asked Ottawa to stop taxing gold, authorize the province to levy its own sales tax and give it a guaranteed annual subsidy, have regional tariffs adjusted to compensate British Columbia for tariff inequalities and freight rates and, last but not least, allow the province to absorb the Canadian National Railways into its own Pacific Great Eastern system.

Pattullo marshalled facts and figures to show that British Columbia had been grossly neglected during the Confederation she had so freely entered. Needless to say, he became highly indignant when the Conservative government in Ottawa sent him home empty-handed. There were mutterings in the province about R. B. Bennett's high-handedness and the word "secession" was frequently murmured in some of Victoria's best drawing-rooms.

Some of Pattullo's thunder dispersed when Mackenzie King became prime minister in 1935. Although a Liberal-to-Liberal conflict was in the offing, Mackenzie King skilfully managed to avoid both confrontation and decision by calling a federal–provincial conference for the end of that year. His communion with the spirits must have been excellent at the time, because the conference ended inconclusively and he could put off succeeding ones without weighing down his conscience. The Rowell–Sirois Commission had been formed to examine all aspects of federal and provincial constitutional powers. This was to be the ultimate probe to determine whether the federal government should or should not control the welfare field.

Pattullo's position worsened as the CCF gained strength and the Liberal Party fell to wrangling about whose snout was stuck deepest in the patronage trough. Fortunately for Pattullo, the fibre of the CCF began to weaken as the party developed its own internal troubles. It operated under the motto "Solidarity Tomorrow" rather than "Solidarity Forever."

The CCF's real problem was its beatific leader, the Reverend Robert Connell, a lover of petunias and primroses, in short a Christian gentleman who mingled the liquors of Christ and Karl Marx in his gentle heart. He was the man chosen to lead the proletarian masses in a Pattullo-controlled legislature. Slaughtered more times than the fabled Innocents, he pleased few by his performance and aroused the contempt of two contenders—the Winches, father and son.

Ernest and Harold displayed the horny-handed aggressiveness that sometimes afflicts self-made men. Proud of their working-class background, proud of the docklands that had bred them and happy to proclaim their pride at the drop of an "aitch," nothing could have been as strange to them as the mild-mannered cleric who dreamed of stamens and socialism— and how could Connell have coped with the hobnailed rush of these proletarian workhorses? The only winner of the clash was Thomas Dufferin Pattullo.

In Vancouver–Burrard, a critical by-election was to be fought. Liberal J. H. Forester and Lyle Telford, the recently elected leader of the CCF, both tangled for the seat. Telford had participated in a purge of Connell and his followers at the CCF convention. But Connell had riposted with a hasty letter to the convention chairman condemning Telford's policies and claiming that the Winches, who backed Telford, were about to plunge the party into a Communist alliance.

That letter played a key part in the Liberal campaign. Pattullo flooded the riding with cabinet ministers and came down himself to echo their assertions that Connell, a likeable, gentle man and a decent soul, had been eliminated by "the all-powerful inside junta which cuts off the political heads of those who disagree with it. . . . If such a body were in absolute control governmentally in this country it is equally certain that off would go many physical heads." Forester beat Telford by 700 votes.

In the Okanagan, Cecil Bennett watched Pattullo's performance and learned from him how to handle the socialists. The premier had found the Achilles heel, the vulnerable spot of the CCF. He had exploited the split within the party between those who represented the will of the working class and were dedicated to change by any means and those intellectuals who wanted change within the system. It was a split that would work to socialism's disadvantage for years to come.

The Vancouver–Burrard by-election was Pattullo's last great stand. The following year, he was forced to back-track on the controversial medicare bill and, while doing so, lost the confidence of George Weir, provincial secretary and minister of education. He skirmished with oil company barons over the regulation of gasoline prices, and while he gained exploration rights for the province he also met hostility from sections of the influential business community. It became apparent even to his most loyal supporters that in his somewhat erratic charge toward "socialized capitalism" he had exposed himself to the danger of losing his right flank to the Conservatives and his left to the CCF. But Pattullo ignored warnings by the pro-Liberal press; nor did he listen to voices within the party itself. He was losing ground, and the man who was panting close behind him was Harold Winch, now openly master of the CCF.

Still undecided as to his course of action, Pattullo went to Ottawa in January 1941 to attend the federal-provincial conference on the findings of the Rowell-Sirois Commission. He would have liked to have grabbed the headlines, but the papers were too full of the Nazi blitz on England. It so happened that Pattullo did get his chance shortly thereafter. For, while in Ottawa, he fell in with Mitch Hepburn, the Liberal premier of Ontario, and William Aberhart, the former messiah and continuing premier of Alberta. The three intensely disliked the commission's recommendations, and Hepburn added pepper to the pot by expressing his loathing for Mackenzie King, his spiritualism and the political sagacity of his dog.

At the conference, Pattullo joined Hepburn and Aberhart in lambasting Mackenzie King. He said he deplored the fact that British Columbia had been called "an eternal drain on Confederation," and he thundered at the delegates in a style reminiscent of the tongue-lashings poor Reverend Connell had received. His province, he said, "did not want to be pushed down to the bottom or even halfway, to tread the treadmill of mediocrity for evermore." He then followed Hepburn's example by quibbling about the agenda for the meeting.

On the second morning of the conference the three appeared bright and early; so did Mackenzie King, who asked them if they were now prepared to seriously discuss the report. The three premiers stomped out of the conference room and informed all and sundry that they had been locked out by the prime minister. But to most observers, it seemed as if Hepburn, Aberhart and Pattullo had walked out on Mackenzie King.

When Pattullo returned home, he was received by angry boards of trade and chambers of commerce, and by irate labour unions as well. They had recommended earlier what the commission had already reported. Pattullo was tired by then, his sense of action had grown flabby and he had trodden down too many paths, veered too many times. Only the most fawning of his political friends remained around him.

As 1941 rolled toward a summer election, he rallied briefly, bringing down a budget which waved a substantial olive branch at Ottawa. But it was not enough. When the election results came in, the Liberals were down to twenty-one seats, four short of majority; the CCF had doubled its standing to fourteen, and the Conservatives, rejuvenated but still backward-looking, had gained twelve; one of them was filled by a chubby, smiling fellow from South Okanagan.

As MY FAMILY was still young, I could not have run for public office sooner. Also, my finances had to be in good order before I could enter politics, because I knew I'd give all my time to it. I had always taken a great interest in all Conservative politics. In 1938, I attended a federal Conservative convention in Ottawa and took my second son Bill with me. Bill was six years old when he attended his first political convention.

I had been trying to get the government to finance some power development in British Columbia. We also needed highways and schools. But I was not having any success convincing anyone. That was when I decided to run. In 1941, there was a provincial election and I felt the time was ripe to throw my hat into the ring. I sought and managed to secure the Conservative nomination in the riding of South Okanagan, which once had been Conservative, but for the last eight years had been a Liberal constituency. The sitting member was Captain Cecil Bull. I wasn't opposed to him personally, as he was a very fine person. Never in my life have I fought an *individual*, per se; I only fought *principles* and *policies*, and I never let anything become personal. By hating somebody, you don't actually hurt that person, as you are the only one who knows about it. Hatred will eat you up inside and destroy you. It is hatred that destroys most politicians. I did not hate Captain Bull, I was merely opposed to his government.

T. D. Pattullo was the Liberal premier of British Columbia. Together with Socred premier William Aberhart of Alberta and Ontario Liberal premier Mitch Hepburn, he had walked out of a federal–provincial conference in Ottawa in 1941. I didn't agree with that. You should have the right to differ, differ strongly and powerfully, but you don't walk out of a conference.

Ottawa had come up with the Rowell–Sirois Report, a

national study about the economic situation in all parts of
Canada. It painted a very dismal picture of British Columbia.
With all its mountains and all its problems, the province
wasn't viable according to the Rowell–Sirois Commission. Of
course I didn't agree with that, so I entered public life.

The main issue I brought up was the report. I condemned
it. I condemned the British Columbia Liberals and the Alberta
Socreds and the Ontario Liberals for walking out of that conference, instead of fighting it out on the floor. What it was all
about was centralization—to centralize everything in Ottawa.
Of course you always have some provinces that want to have a
strong central government, and federal socialists want to have
a strong central government because they want to plan everybody's lives, and they can only do that from the centre. I was
opposed to all those things.

As far as the report's views on British Columbia were
concerned, I had the answers, and I voiced them very clearly.
They became the promises I later carried out. We had no highways, not even simple trails. We needed highways. We had
terrible, unpaved roads. We lacked bridges and tunnels. We
lacked proper ferries at the coast. We lacked power and hydro-
electric stations, which could create jobs and industry. We
were in a terrible mess. The poor and the old needed looking
after; where was our welfare system? It was on all these issues
that I fought the election and got elected to the British Columbia provincial legislature. It was a very close race. I had about
130 votes more than my Liberal opponent who came in second;
the CCFer, a nice lady, came in third.

The rules that I set up then I carried out during all of the
thirty-two years I was an MLA. One of them was that our stores
would not sell supplies, either directly or indirectly, to any
government department. I wrote a letter to the purchasing
commission in Victoria informing them that they were not to
buy at Bennett's stores. Then I wrote to individual government
departments, stating that if any mistakes were made, and
something *was* indeed sold, they were not to pay for the
merchandise.

Before we had a bridge, the Kelowna ferry ran across Lake Okanagan. The previous owners of my store had done all the work on the ferry and the ferry people were used to coming to us to buy their supplies. After I became an MLA, I told them I was very sorry, but we couldn't serve them any more.

They replied, "Oh, certainly you can serve us, because what we need isn't available anywhere else. If you don't sell to us, the ferry service will be held up." One day one of my staff sold something to them and when I found out about it, I asked that the merchandise be taken off the ferry. I then refunded the money; it was quite a scene. As a result the ferry was grounded for a while, but I had obeyed one of my own rules.

I'm proud of my first motion in the Liberal–Conservative coalition. It was to ask for an increase in the federal old age pension, which, at the time, was a mere $20 per month.

My motion passed caucus. Some people wanted to use the money for other purposes, but I was joined by a Liberal, who seconded the motion, and it was carried. We were criticized by others in the legislature, and Mr. Pattullo said we were taking the federal government off the hook. I told him that wasn't the way to look at federal–provincial co-operation. "You don't hurt the people, especially the old who were the pioneers, because of some federal–provincial disagreement. Just because some politician is playing partisan politics, there is no excuse for not doing the right thing. Let it be on his conscience, not on yours."

I believed a true Conservative to be a person who, when he saw a tree on fire, would cut off the smouldering branch to save the tree. In the Okanagan Valley, where there are different orchards, you have to prune trees. You'd think you'd kill them, you have to prune them so much; but pruning makes them healthier. That's what you've got to do with economic and political systems; cut government spending and allow free enterprise.

My whole idea has always been to build the Conservative Party into a genuine *free* enterprise party, a genuine *competitive* enterprise party, a party without patronage, which not only sponsors development and promotes balanced budgets, but also works toward great social reform. I believe that private enterprise can bring about that social reform better than any socialist system can. But the Conservatives were controlled by small financial groups on Toronto's Bay Street and in Montreal. As they didn't want anybody to rock the boat, they looked at me as if I were a radical within their ranks. They didn't want reforms because they didn't like to pay taxes. I told them they wouldn't have to pay more taxes if we had development together with reforms. You can't have reforms without development; that's where the socialists are wrong. They believe in no-growth policies. If there's no growth, you can't afford to give people social benefits. But if development is on a sound basis, you can have reforms and the economy can finance them at the same time. For me that was easy to see, but those stupid Tories couldn't see it. I fought them at every federal convention, and I also fought for the Tory leadership in British Columbia.

In 1941, when I was elected Conservative MLA, the Liberals had lost their majority; they threw out Pattullo and went into coalition with the Conservatives. I was in favour of this coalition, as it was not right for the provinces to spend large sums of money on political in-fighting when it could be put to better use to help the war effort. I insisted that we offer the same arrangement to the CCF, but they rejected it. However, when the war was over, I demanded that we make up for the lost years and get our economy into high gear. We had been deprived of productivity because of the Depression, and precious time had been lost due to the Second World War.

During those early days we had good coalition government. John Hart, the Liberal leader, was premier. Pat Maitland, a prominent lawyer, was Conservative leader and attorney-general. He died in the spring of 1946 and then, in December 1947, John Hart resigned. The government changed and the old patronage machine which we had abolished was back.

As a Conservative, I felt it was my duty to first clean up my own party as far as I could. I had a group of young men—

Judge Bewley, Robert Bonner who eventually became my attorney-general—all those were young Conservatives in those days; there were a dozen or more, we were quite a force. We forced an election for the leadership, and thought we had it won. But the Conservative political machine moved in with its delegates, and we lost. We didn't give up. We tried it again, and lost a second time the same way. The machine was too strong.

I'd been a Conservative all my life. I felt that I owed it to my party and myself, that I'd first try to clean up the Conservative Party before I would leave it. And I did try. I went back into the legislature and still fought for development. But they always said, "Next year; we have no money, no money, no money, no money."

There was a federal vacancy in the Okanagan Valley in what they called the Yale riding. Grote Stirling, a wonderful person, had been Conservative member there for years. I had supported him and campaigned with him during every election. In 1948, he was a sick man and didn't want to run. I said to him, "You can run but you can't campaign. I'll do all the campaigning for you as a provincial member." Federally, Okanagan was a much bigger riding than provincially, with Kelowna at its core. I campaigned for Grote and he got in, of course, but mainly because of his name. Shortly after being elected, he died. Now there were vacancies in two constituencies, one Liberal seat in Ontario and another one in the Conservative constituency of Yale. There were going to be two by-elections.

A person I strongly supported was John Bracken, leader of the national Conservative Party. He had been premier of Manitoba; a tremendous person. The Conservatives are always after their leader, and they were after him. He told me, "The enemies are within the party, and if I lose this by-election, they'll move in. I want you to run, W.A.C."

Then other federal Conservatives came to me, including Howard Green and John Diefenbaker. I said, "The CCF have a little wave across Canada now, in '48. All we've got to do is split the free-enterprise vote, and you're going to have CCF members elected in Yale and in Ontario." They realized that as well.

Then Howard Green came back to tell me that an arrangement had been made with C. D. Howe, the Liberal reconstruction minister in Ottawa, that if I ran in Yale the Liberals would not oppose me. In return, the Conservatives would not oppose the Liberal candidate in the Ontario by-election. I accepted the nomination on that basis and things got going nicely.

C. D. Howe and Howard Green were fine men, but they were very stubborn. One day they got into a fight in Parliament, and after that the deal was off. So the Liberals picked E. J. Chambers, head of the fruit industry and a wonderful chap, to run as their best candidate in Yale riding, and the Conservatives picked somebody else to run in the by-election in Ontario.

Of course, Mr. Chambers didn't know about the previous arrangements that had been made, or he would never have entered the race. I know, because in the dying days of the election campaign, he came to me and said, "W. A. C., I'm stupid to be in this fight. I just found out that we're going to cancel each other out, and a CCF man will be elected." I realized that it was a little late to do much about it but told him we would have to go through with it anyway. When the votes were counted, the CCF got most of them. They won and I came in second, and the Liberals were third. Incidentally, the CCF also won in Ontario.

I'm a great believer that everything eventually turns out for the best. That election was a great experience for me. Not only that, but now nobody in British Columbia could come to me and say, "Why don't you run federally, why don't you run federally?" I could always say, "I did offer myself."

I don't want to boast, but I believe that if I had been elected, then in due time I would have been prime minister of Canada. And I'm sure Canada wouldn't be in the financial mess it's got into since.

Bennett's return to provincial politics put a burr under Herbert Anscomb's saddle. The querulous and magisterial leader of the Conservatives could hardly welcome the man who had tried out for his job in 1946, after Royal "Pat" Maitland's death. Since then, as finance minister, a portfolio that carried a reasonable flow of patronage, Anscomb had been consolidating his grip not only on the party but on the coalition itself.

Three years had passed since that "brash fellow" from South Okanagan had persuaded Tilly Rolston to nominate him for the leadership. Mrs. Rolston, a woman of ample dimensions and convictions to match, had accommodated W. A. C. Bennett because he had promised to rectify the lack of Tory ladies in the coalition cabinet. Anscomb had crushed this attempt at premature feminism, declaring that the real issue between him and the "cheeky chap" from Kelowna was that *he* was supporting the Conservative Party, whereas Bennett was set on fusing the Conservatives and the Liberals into a permanent coalition. Despite Bennett's denials, Anscomb won. It was true that Bennett had fed the "fusion" idea to the *Province* and the *Victoria Times*, but only, he claimed, to draw attention to himself and his ideas.

Now Anscomb was ready to leap into Government House and walk out as premier of the province. But the Liberals had endured him too long. True, the coalition had to stay, as it was the only way to keep the Socialist "menace" at bay—not to mention all the other dangers that threatened "Patronage Paradise." But Anscomb as premier would corrode even a cast-iron Liberal stomach. Instead, they chose Bjorn Ingemar Johnson, a harmless man, to be their new leader over the claims of Gordon Wismer, who in 1937, during his term as attorney-general, had created the Vancouver–Centre political machine— a machine, Blair Fraser said, that "shared the gamiest reputation in Canada" with Montreal–Cartier.

Liberals and Conservatives faced each other like two dogs wanting to occupy the same fire hydrant. The Liberals knew that Anscomb would prefer to end the coalition if it meant he could grab power, while Anscomb and his Tories knew that the Liberals were preparing to break the loving cup as soon as circumstances would allow it. Indeed, Arthur Laing, the new Liberal Party president, had told the delegates at the convention, "I don't favour breaking up the coalition tomorrow but I shall go to every Liberal association in this province and do all I can to put Liberalism first in British Columbia."

In the end, the sweetheart arrangement endured. Neither side could risk letting in the CCF and both needed the strings of patronage their mutual bargain had brought them. With them they rolled into the 1949 election trailing the usual stream of promises: greater development, massive expansion, more roads, more railways, more money to be spent everywhere. In unison with these promissory fanfares went the rattle of sabres, the swift swords of the Cold War warriors, ever ready to cut down the Reds. Horror stories were told of the deplorable conditions prevailing in Socialist Britain and "Red" Saskatchewan; rumours were spread about secret deals between the Labour Progressive Party, the new title for the Communist Party, and the CCF. The atmosphere grew so tense, in fact, that the CCF decided to stop singing "The Red Flag," a tradition at their meetings. However, they did have to sing it once, when an organist was bribed by a local Conservative to play it.

The old scare techniques worked. The coalition swept to victory, the Liberals picking up the seven seats they needed to gain a majority, leaving the Conservatives in a minority situation.

The party that Bennett rejoined had not looked so dilapidated since the declining days of Simon Fraser Tolmie. Its provincial base was tucked away in the high-income district of Vancouver and the affluent rural area of the Fraser Valley. Beyond those ridings, Anscomb held Oak Bay as the sole Conservative seat on Vancouver Island; Lillooet, Salmon Arm, Mackenzie and South Okanagan held out amid a sea of Liberals and CCFers.

The Conservative party faithfuls muttered about Liberals raiding weakened Conservative ridings. Howard Green and David Fulton, two federal Tories who had survived the Liberal onslaught in the 1949 federal election, met with David Tupper and Robert Bonner and other young Conservatives to form the "Action Club" in which the name of "Anscomb" was anathematized over glasses of whiskey. Tilly Rolston held tea parties and wept to her friends about Anscomb's blind anti-feminism, stating how sick she was of watching her women colleagues lick envelopes while Liberal women were invited to sit in the cabinet.

W. A. C. Bennett offered himself as the magnet that could attract all the disaffected elements. He had listened to the promises and the hollow phrases expounded in the Speech from the Throne, knowing full well that nothing would be done for the interior of the province where he and thousands of others lived. It still took hours to travel the thirty miles from Vernon to Kelowna. The Pacific Great Eastern was still stalled at Squamish, hundreds of miles north of its promised terminus in North Vancouver. Irrigation projects had dried out for lack of funding. Bennett was sick of a government that only catered to big business development and forgot about the little man. He became a lonely man indeed when one day he even went so far as to vote with the CCF on a labour bill.

While the anti-Anscomb forces gathered, Bennett toured the province, listening to complaints from Cariboo, Kootenay, Vancouver Island and the lower mainland. He knew that the coalition was in trouble no matter how many times Anscomb and Johnson shook each other's hands. A socialist victory was unavoidable unless one party or the other rejuvenated itself. Bennett therefore made a bid for the Conservative leadership at the Tory convention in October 1950.

The trouble was that it was not a leadership convention. Strictly speaking, a new leader can only be chosen if the old one first resigns. Anscomb was in no mood to relinquish power, and so the convention turned into a vicious brawl. W. A. C. Bennett attacked him for continuing to be owner and director of Grower's Wine and Coast Breweries Limited. Though Anscomb had, in fact, declined the attorney-generalship because the post dealt with liquor offences, he couldn't see why a finance minister should not purchase supplies from his own companies. He defended his actions as sound business practices and thought it was in bad taste to raise the issue, describing it as factionalist. Somehow, he managed to swing the convention around, finally taking the vote by 453 to 167.

In victory, Anscomb remained as ungenerous as ever, refusing Bennett's offer to make the vote unanimous. He then advised the delegates to look around for a stable young man to eventually take his place, as he was getting on in years.

The time had come for Cecil Bennett to assess his situation. He knew he had the support of Tilly Rolston and the members of the Conservative Action Club, as well as of Judge Lew Bewley and the Young Conservatives. Yet, after ten years in politics, he was as far removed from the front bench as he had ever been. He had built a prosperous business and was considered a successful man. But in Victoria he was just that maverick who could do nothing but criticize. But how could he hold back when the new session was unearthing monumental incompetency in handling government funds?

The major crisis of the new session was the muddle in the British Columbia Hospital Insurance Service. Deficits were running at close to $5 million, as thousands of subscribers defaulted on their payments. The health minister was lying in one of his own hospitals, having suffered a heart attack brought on by the crisis in his department.

Finance Minister Anscomb advised Premier Johnson to raise insurance premiums. It was an echo of a speech he had made during the Depression advising Pattullo to cut welfare payments to the bone and then "carve the bone." His 1951 speech had much the same effect as his earlier one: the people were enraged. Johnson brought in a bill to raise the ceiling on hospital premium payments. In addition, patients would have to pay $3.50 for each of their first ten days in hospital.

To Cecil Bennett, this was no solution at all, and he said so very plainly inside the House. They may not have paid much attention to him there, but on the outside thousands did. He received letters from several riding associations congratulating him on his principled stand against raising the premium ceiling.

The crisis in the hospital service reached such proportions that Vancouver General would not admit a patient until $35 had been collected. This was news fit to print. The papers hammered away, but Bennett realized that it was also symptomatic of a sickness that was far more severe. People were beginning to distrust the coalition and dislike the old labels. There were many of them out there—small-town lawyers, realtors, small-time loggers, farmers, dentists, hardware merchants—people like himself. They were outsiders denied access to the inner circles of power, barred from running the old parties but too wary of the perils of socialism to vote CCF.

W. A. C. Bennett saw the present government as a business enterprise that had lost the confidence of the shareholders. The time seemed right to take a more decisive step and he was ready to take it.

I WAS HATED terribly as a Conservative MLA. During the war I had not found fault with the provincial government for not doing much in B.C. It was right at a time when we were fighting for life and country. But once the war was over and the veterans were returning home, I wanted to see some action.

By 1951, I'd been a Conservative member for ten years. I'd never mentioned to anyone that I was dissatisfied with the coalition; not even to Tilly Rolston, my good friend from Point Grey, who was also disillusioned. She wanted to walk the floor, but at the time her mind wasn't completely made up, and besides, her strong allegiance to Conservatism held her back. Tilly was as much in the dark as everybody else about my intentions to walk the floor. She knew that I was dissatisfied, that's all.

I remember that day in March 1951 when I stood up in the House right after prayers and said, "Madam Speaker, I no longer have confidence in the Liberals, the Conservatives, or the coalition government, and I now disassociate myself from the coalition government, both in this House and throughout this province. I call on this government to resign because it has changed since the days of Hart and Maitland, when it was the best government British Columbia ever had. So I wish to advise you that from now on I shall sit in this House as the member for South Okanagan, but as an independent member." I then nodded to the Speaker, left the House and went uptown to see a show.

That same night, I went back to the House to find out where my seat was. I found it; they'd put me right behind the CCF. Oh yes, they tried to make things difficult for me, but in effect they had made them easy. I sat so close to some CCF members that I could just lean forward and suggest things to them. Then they'd get up and say what I had suggested.

The press wrote, "Bennett's finished, he's walked out into oblivion, he's too smart for himself, he's out, we'll hear no more from him!" But I knew when I walked the floor that we would start something, a movement of some kind, and I also knew that I would lead it.

After that, I made some strenuous efforts to persuade Mrs. Rolston to walk the floor. She had been hoping that the government would come up with something constructive, anything that would further the cause of British Columbia. The Liberals and the Conservatives knew that she was dissatisfied;

they promised her everything, if she would only stay. And soon they thought they had got around her. But she astounded all of them when, about ten days later, she too walked the floor. I had suggested what words she should use on that day in the House. Tilly Rolston was a wonderful, strong-minded, fine person.

Then I took a trip across Canada to study the political situation. Although I saw *some* good things everywhere, I found that the Social Credit government in Alberta was head and shoulders above any other system at that time. I know that my critics always had difficulty understanding why I joined the Social Credit Party after having been a life-long Conservative. I did it because I believed in the basic principles of the movement. Social Credit means just one thing, "That which is physically possible, desirable and morally right, must be made financially possible."

If I had stayed and served the Conservative Party, my critics would have praised me to the skies; if I had stayed in the coalition with the Liberals, they also would have praised me; and if I had crossed the floor and joined the socialists, they all would have cried "Hallelujah!" But wading into cold, unfamiliar waters, joining Social Credit, a party which had never won a single seat in British Columbia, was walking into oblivion. When our critics developed phrases such as "funny money" and "those Bible-punching bunch of Social Crediters," I said to them, "First of all, what's wrong with the Bible? Isn't it the foundation of our civilization, as we know it till now? What funny money? The only funny part is that Social Credit is the one party, the one government that has always paid its debts." Social Credit believes in balanced budgets, in pay as you go—all those things I had always believed in.

When I joined the Social Credit Party in December 1951, I joined it as a private citizen. I had no assurances of any kind, no promises of getting nominated anywhere; I had to fight all the way. The socialists were against me, although they had been my friends when I walked the floor; but when I became a Socred, they suddenly were my enemies. Of course, all my

Tory friends were mad at me, and so were my Liberal friends, with whom we had been in coalition. Even most of the Socreds thought I had been planted by the Conservatives. "Let's stop W. A. C.," they said. I don't think the people in Alberta really wanted me to be the leader in British Columbia. And, of course, the press was totally opposed to me.

In fact, I had no support from anyone. When I got up in the House at the first session in March of 1952, catcalls came from everywhere: "What is Social Credit?"

After I got them to be quiet for a minute or two, I tried to explain that the movement doesn't compare with Christianity, and that I was not going to say it does. "But what is Christianity?" I asked. "To the Greeks it was stupidity, to the Jews it was a stumbling block, but to those who believed in it, it was life eternal. And to the socialists, to the Liberal and the Conservative patronage-bound parties, Social Credit is craziness, it's stupid and it's a stumbling block. But for the ordinary people of British Columbia it will mean great progress, development, a higher standard of living, social reform and a government that's out of debt."

~ 5 ~

Going Like Wildfire

Social Credit was started in British Columbia by three men. They met quietly in 1932 in Vancouver's Shell Building; Henry Torey and William Rose were reporters for the *Sun*, which owned the building, and the third man was William A. Tutte, a West Coast fetishist of sorts.

The three emerged with an aim. They would spread the teachings of Major Douglas throughout British Columbia under the quasi-military name of the Douglas Social Credit Group, British Columbia Section. By 1934, through their efforts, the Kiwanis Club was able to muster one thousand people to listen to Major Douglas address a dinner meeting at the Hotel Vancouver. The ladies in the audience were enthralled, for as the *Province* said the next day, "The Major spoke in the deep intonations of a cultured Briton."

The Major's theories, obscure though they may have sounded, appealed to his audiences' deep-seated suspicions. He would expound the "A + B" theorem, one of the pillars of his ideology. "A" was the payments made to individuals through salaries, wages and dividends, "B" the external costs such as bank charges and cost of materials that went into making a product. The price of the product was the sum of "A + B."

Then Major Douglas would pause to let the import of his message sink in. Slowly, it would dawn on his audience that "A" alone could not possibly pay for the goods the workers were producing. How would they buy them? "Yes," the Major would pick up, "they need credit." And where would they get credit? Who would get richer as the producer became poorer consuming what he had produced? From within, the people in the audience would hear the razor-edged voices of their own fears. "The banks, the credit institutions, the loan corporations are run for profit without any sense for the common good." A light would go on in the minds of the small businessmen who were listening. These were the people who depended on extended credit as a lifeline. But in 1934, the banks were reeling in those lifelines, repossessing property, confiscating the assets that had been lavished on building up a business. Major Douglas' appeal fell on fertile ground, and despite the scorn that poured in from academic economists, despite the mockery of "liberal" thinkers, the born-again Social Crediter marched on, cherishing the mockery and relishing the scorn. For there was a tinge of fundamentalist religion to his beliefs: "Blessed are they who suffer for the new economic institution's sake."

The next year—1935—the religious hue purpled when the Very Reverend Dr. Hewlett Johnson, Dean of Canterbury, not yet the Red Dean, came to bless the Social Credit colours. He sounded the organ tones of High Anglicanism over the hushed multitude. "I am a socialist at heart," he said, "a liberal with my head and a conservative in my bones. And Social Credit appeals to my heart, head and bones."

The euphoria lasted through the Aberhart victory in Alberta until the spring of 1936, when a new organization was formed that would combine monetary reform with a bid for political power—the Social Credit League of British Columbia gave up the revolutionary dreams of the Douglas Social Credit Group to contest the 1937 election. Into its ranks came William Aberhart, dreaming of a drive on Ottawa after consolidating his hold on the West. He secretly visited various British Columbian dissidents and urged them to form groups loyal to the Alberta movement. Several months later, in September 1936, he appeared publicly in Vancouver and Victoria, exhorting the League to unify and allow him to lead it up Parliament Hill. The result was a new organization, in addition to the League, that called itself the British Columbia Social Credit Union; it was run in the province by John Loveseth, but it was actually controlled from Alberta.

William Aberhart could behave with all the high-handedness of an Old Testament prophet because he was, in fact, the confirmed and sole disciple of Major Douglas. The circumstances that brought him the Major's imprimatur make a strange story.

Back in 1935, when Aberhart and Social Credit had ridden the whirlwind into the Alberta legislature, repercussions were felt within the Social Credit leadership in Great Britain. The mover and shaker within the hierarchy was a character straight out of Kipling called John Hargrave, a man with a knack for forming movements out of the miasmas of various theories. His first venture had been a folk-revival movement called the "Kibbo Kif," an old Cheshire phrase for "strong and hearty." The members of this oddly named group yearned to return to the heyday of stout British yeomanry, with a sniff of G. K. Chesterton's resolute march back to the Middle Ages. But also present was more than a hint of the same urge that drove Heinrich Himmler and his minions to commune at the tombs of dead German emperors, clad in fancy-dress.

The Kibbo Kif met on holt and heath, wearing the hooded cowls of Anglo–Saxon peasantry together with Prussian military cloaks. They sat around campfires imploring natural energy forces to make them as keen as Sheffield steel and as hard as the granite of the Pennines. These "wild men" were supported by eminently respectable people such as H. G. Wells.

John Hargrave read Douglas' articles in *The New Age* and became enamoured of the "A + B" theorem. The Kibbo Kif were exhorted to throw off their cowls and cloaks, put on the green shirts of Social Credit and march through the streets. They brawled and ran soup kitchens for the hungry just as the Fascists and the Communists were doing. These were the thirties, when rationalists got their eyes blacked unless the "wild men" who sang songs of economic reform applauded them.

Then the news came of Aberhart's victory in Alberta. Hargrave surveyed his serried ranks and concluded that there must be yet another change. His fighting formations were abandoned and the green shirts were exchanged for sober business suits and rolled umbrellas. The "wild men" became members of the Social Credit Party of Great Britain, campaigning in the 1935 elections. They ran and they lost—totally.

Hargrave began to nurse the suspicion that Aberhart in his winning efforts had perverted Social Credit. Obviously he had become the tool of the dreaded financiers. Hargrave set his findings before Major Douglas, who suggested that Hargrave go to Alberta to set Aberhart on the true path once again.

What John Hargrave did not know was that Douglas wanted to be rid of him. The Major, having noticed that Hargrave was goose-stepping down the same path as the National Socialists in Germany, wanted none of that for Social Credit.

Secretly, he advised Aberhart that Hargrave was not to be trusted, discrediting any connection with the movement Hargrave might lay claim to.

Yet despite the boost he had received from Douglas, Aberhart lost control of the British Columbia Social Credit Union. Mr. Lund, a member of Aberhart's advisory board, denounced him as another Mussolini, and the Union's recording secretary, Mrs. M. Bower Hopkinson, sued him for $500 in back wages she claimed he had never paid her.

In the 1937 elections, the Social Credit League captured less than 1 percent of the vote, and in the years that followed became little more than a showcase for a variety of deranged talents. There emerged the British Israelites and those who saw a Zionist conspiracy everywhere; jovial, pixilated money reformers who drew moral support from the beer taps at the Canadian Legion halls, and zealots who had only recently abandoned flat earth theories to embrace the Douglas principles of money reform.

Solon Low, the Mormon head of the Social Credit Association of Canada, appeared in 1944 to pull the League together by giving it the new name of Social Credit Association of Canada (British Columbia Section). But he ruined his efforts by putting the ineffectual Major Andrew Henry Jukes, DSO, OBE, late of the Ninth Gurkha Rifles, at the helm. Jukes' mind did not move; it remained petrified in the strata of the extreme right. He led the Association in British Columbia by taking his share of its funds and running for cover whenever work or a fresh idea presented itself.

Two men then made an effort to push Social Credit onto the road to recovery; one was Peer Paynter, a farmer and carpenter from Saskatchewan who had once been accused of being a Communist by one of the wilder Social Crediters. Solon Low himself later cleared him of that charge. The other man was Lyle Wicks, a Vancouver street railwayman who one day had stood waiting for a bus with Fred Mix, a fellow-worker and a Social Crediter. "There's no reason why a man should have to stand fifteen minutes waiting for a bus," said Mix. "Why can't we have more buses?" With these remarks, Mix created a magic formula in Wicks' mind. He promptly equated Social Credit with buses, a subject dear to his heart. "I saw," said Wicks later, "that this is what we had been waiting for. We are headed for a slave state unless Social Credit cures the evil in our midst."

Wicks and Paynter rose in the Social Credit Association.

By 1948, with the blessings of Solon Low, the federal executive and the "high command" of Alberta, they were preparing to steal the Association from the egregious Jukes who, although lazy, erratic and totally insensitive to political realities, was out to prove that he was still running things. By calling a national convention, he stole a march on the Paynter–Wicks coalition, as he could pack it with his own supporters.

Although Wicks and Paynter lost their seats on the executive, they soon held their own convention, during which they formed the British Columbia Social Credit League. It had only 400 members, but its financial base was secure, as Alberta had promised to fund it. In the 1949 provincial election, the League fielded sixteen candidates, while Jukes had eleven candidates contesting seats mainly in Vancouver and the Islands. The League platform was curiously devoid of old Social Credit slogans; there was no mention of the "A + B" theorem, no talk of scrip money, no mention of a Zionist conspiracy and not a single British Israelite was in sight. Instead, the League called for reform and a true free enterprise system.

But this new moderation failed to gain support, as Conservative Anscomb and Liberal Johnson, working the old magic created by Hart and Maitland, swept back into power. Paradoxically, Social Credit gained strength following that election. Alberta stood behind the League, happy to pour in funds against the day when Social Credit would come to power in British Columbia and Alberta would collect the notes with interest.

There were thousands of ex-Albertans in the interior of British Columbia, religious fundamentalists homesteading on the new frontier and heeding the words of Alberta's Premier Ernest Manning, who spoke to them each morning over the radio. There were Catholics in Nelson–Creston and Rossland–Trail who were looking for government aid for their schools and found that the Socreds were listening. Small loggers shut out by the big companies, notaries public quashed by big lawyers, and board of trade members exploited by the powerful with friends in Victoria discovered that the League cared about them. It gathered them in and signed them up. For the first time in its strife-torn history the movement changed its name without a crisis, calling itself the Social Credit Party of British Columbia. Between April 1949 and the fall of 1950, its membership trebled.

Prominent Alberta politicians toured the province, touting

Social Credit—Orvis Kennedy, the national organizer in Edmonton; Reverend Ernest Hansell, cartoonist, preacher and member for McLeod; David Ure, Alberta's minister of agriculture. They penetrated the Kootenays, the Cariboo and the Okanagan with their message. "Not oil," David Ure told his listeners, "but a good, honest Christian government has made Alberta. . . . All you need for a government in British Columbia is a dozen honest men. You are loaded with wealth. Why don't you keep some yourself?"

The strategy began to pay off. There were defections from Tory and Grit ranks. Liberals Ronald Worley and J. Donald Smith met with Hansell and Kennedy, then announced their new allegiance to Social Credit. W. G. Gillard, past president of the South Okanagan Progressive Conservative Association, joined; so did Tom Bate, head of the Dunbar Division of the Point Grey Progressive Conservative Association in Tilly Rolston's riding; G. L. Beyerstein, a prominent lumber operator in Cranbrook; K. R. Blain, who owned a store in Kimberley and was a local alderman.

Although these men added lustre to the cause, none could take star billing. The party needed a name that was known across the province; William Chant, a former Alberta cabinet minister and retired farmer, combined with Worley, Smith and Bate to propose W. A. C. Bennett. Here, they argued, was a man of ability, with ten years in government; a man of principle, and the first to abandon the ill-fated coalition. He alone had stood for the tenets of decency. "We need him," they said, "Social Credit needs him, British Columbia needs him."

Then dissenting voices arose, mainly from the Alberta wing. J. A. Reid, a sawmill operator from Salmon Arm, who claimed to be one of the "Sacred Twelve" who had first supported Aberhart, pointed out Bennett's lack of Social Credit pedigree. To him, W. A. C. was merely another renegade Tory ready to turn again when the tide changed. Peer Paynter and Hugh L. Shantz, a Vernon grocer and director of Youth for Christ, backed Reid. Their feelings were known and shared by the one and true Alberta Temple. The Albertans had ideas of their own, and to control British Columbia was only the first. Once they had consolidated their hold from the Prairies to the Pacific, they hoped to force Ottawa to implement the monetary reforms necessary to make Social Credit a reality right across the country.

At first, Bennett was snubbed by Paynter and his group;

they did not invite him to attend the November convention in New Westminster. He went home to think things over. On December 6, 1951, he announced that he had taken out membership in the Kelowna Association of the Social Credit Party. He carried on his apostolate from his vantage point in Victoria, the centre of provincial political action. People came there to air their grievances, among them a delegation to protest the building of a reservoir that fed the gigantic Alcan aluminum smelters at Burns Lake near Kitimat. The farmers were up in arms because both the water table and the beautiful shoreline of the lake had been devastated. None was more angry than Cyril Shelford, the young man who had been chosen to head the group.

UP IN KITIMAT, they'd had some terrible arguments with the Aluminum Company of Canada. The old Conservative government had given the company special land concessions, and the farmers were aroused about that. In 1952, as a Social Credit member, I received many telegrams asking me to fly up to Kitimat to meet the people, listen to their problems and help them out. I wired back, "A waste of money." Instead, I proposed they come to Victoria when the legislature was in session and I'd do anything I could, even though I was only one voice in opposition.

They arrived, Shelford among them. First they went to see Harold Winch, the leader of the CCF; then they were received by some Liberal and Conservative members of the coalition, but they never got in to see the cabinet.

When they saw me, I told them to come to my office three times a day and I would be there waiting for them. "It will become known all around that you're in to see me," I said, "and the government will think we are plotting something. I know that they'll see you then."

The plan worked and the Kitimat party was soon called in to meet the cabinet. They had some girls with them; one of them was taking a few notes. She was not supposed to take notes in a meeting of that type. But instead of asking her politely to hand over the notes, they bawled her out, and she started to cry. All this information was leaked to me.

Being in opposition, it was my job to embarrass the government. I got up in the House to tell the story, saying how
terrible it was, given our British parliamentary tradition, that
such a thing had happened to a girl who had never been inside
the parliament buildings before and of course didn't know the
rules. I pointed out that to grab the papers from the girl and
upset her was awful. I cried, "That's no way to treat a citizen,
no matter how strong a government you are. That's what the
people of this province are against; they object to that kind of
leadership. They want a PEOPLE'S government!"

My friends in the government were mad at me and they
were also mad at the people from Kitimat, presumably for
having leaked the story to me. Of course it wasn't Shelford,
but another member of the delegation. In the end, they didn't
get much help from the government, but they got a little, and
before returning to Kitimat Shelford came to see me in my
office. I said to him, "I've done everything I could for you,
now I want you to do one thing for me."

He was eager to listen and I told him that I was about to
address my first Social Credit meeting in Victoria. "Some of
the coalition members are sympathetic to my cause: they will
be there. I'd like you to come too."

They all came, although the meeting was held in a very
small place. Until then I hadn't talked politics to Shelford,
but by the time I had signed him up as a party member and
had given him a small book of tickets, he was very enthusiastic.
"Go back to your riding," I told him, "and sign up enough
members so you can get the nomination papers. Approach
people up and down the street, and you'll be our candidate."

Although the fortunes of Social Credit flourished, the Socreds
were still leaderless early in 1952.

Wicks had repudiated his previous opposition to Bennett,
announcing in January that a convention would be held within
two or three weeks to choose a leader for the British Columbia
party. He affirmed that he had no personal aspirations for
leadership. In fact the convention was not held until the end of

April, and in the interval Wicks was hastily summoned to the inner sanctum of Alberta. Ernest Manning and Solon Low advised him that the Reverend Ernest Hansell, devout anti-Semite and sometime minister in the Church of Christ, was the chosen and soon to be anointed leader of Social Credit in British Columbia and that W. A. C. Bennett was suspect and unreliable.

The April convention became known as the Calgary Stampede. Albertans packed the hall, over-rode all other voices and galloped away with the Reverend Hansell at their head. The old faith had triumphed and Social Credit seemed poised to slide back to those halcyon days of Jew-baiting and superstitions. "Edmonton," said the Vancouver *Province*, "is the chosen city, the mecca of the faithful, and it will be interesting to see Pacific coast cities kneeling on the warm sands at each sunset, salaaming to the east as Manning the Muezzin calls from the minarets of the legislative buildings on the other side of the mountains which, we presume, he will allow to remain where they are."

None of this pleased Bennett very much, but neither did it dismay him. He had hewn to a fine line all through the convention, managing to steer it away from appointing an out-and-out leader. He had supported a move to alter the constitution to allow the selection of a temporary campaign leader instead. He was nominated for that position, together with Chant, Hansell, Solon Low and Paynter. Having assessed his chances and found them shaky, he had declined to stand. Instead Hansell had grabbed the brass ring. Bennett knew that when the voting was over, the man chosen by the party's elected representatives would be the one to wield the true power. South Okanagan would return him, he was sure of that. He had ten years of political experience in the House. When the time came to lead the party into the legislature, Bennett was certain that he would be the man in front.

What Bennett needed now was an election, and Herbert Anscomb gave it to him on a plate. Anscomb went to Ottawa to thunder at the St. Laurent government, demanding the favours British Columbia had never received. To prop up Johnson, the federal Liberals acceded to Anscomb's demands. He whisked back to Victoria, grabbing every reporter within reach.

Premier Johnson had the bilious experience of learning about his government's magnificent new tax-sharing arrangements in that evening's newspapers, which made much of Herbert Anscomb's sagacity. W. A. C. Bennett, standing on the

Cecil Bennett's mother, née Mary Emma Burns, at the age of twenty.

Opposite
Hampton, New Brunswick in 1905.

Mary Emma Bennett, in her fifties, and Cecil Bennett, shortly after his arrival in Edmonton.

Right
The Marshall–Wells building in Edmonton.

Below
The business section of Westlock, Alberta in 1925. Bennett's first hardware store is in the centre of the photograph.

Housez Studios, Edmonton

Socred "funny money" used by the Alberta government. W.A.C.
Bennett's government never issued any in British Columbia.

The Bennett hardware store in Vernon, British Columbia during
"Pioneer Days" in the 1930s.

	AUG. 26. 1936	SEPT. 2. 1936	SEPT. 9. 1936	SEPT. 16. 1936	SEPT. 23. 1936	SEPT. 30. 1936	OCT. 7. 1936	OCT. 14. 1936	OCT. 21. 1936	OCT. 28. 1936	ALBERTA 1 CENT	1 CENT	NOV. 1936
DEC. 2. 1936	DEC. 9. 1936	DEC. 16. 1936	DEC. 23. 1936	DEC. 30. 1936	JAN. 6. 1937	JAN. 13. 1937	JAN. 20. 1937	JAN. 27. 1937	FEB. 3. 1937	FEB. 10. 1937	FEB. 17. 1937	FEB. 24. 1937	MAR. 3. 1937
MAR. 17. 1937	MAR. 24. 1937	MAR. 31. 1937	APRIL 7. 1937	APRIL 14. 1937	APRIL 21. 1937	APRIL 28. 1937	MAY 5. 1937	MAY 12. 1937	MAY 19. 1937	MAY 26. 1937	JUNE 2. 1937	JUNE 9. 1937	JUNE 16. 1937
JUNE 30. 1937	JULY 7. 1937	JULY 14. 1937	JULY 21. 1937	JULY 28. 1937	AUG. 4. 1937	AUG. 11. 1937	AUG. 18. 1937	AUG. 25. 1937	SEPT. 1. 1937	SEPT. 8. 1937	SEPT. 15. 1937	SEPT. 22. 1937	SEPT. 29. 1937
OCT. 13. 1937	OCT. 20. 1937	OCT. 27. 1937	NOV. 3. 1937	NOV. 10. 1937	NOV. 17. 1937	NOV. 24. 1937	DEC. 1. 1937	DEC. 8. 1937	DEC. 15. 1937	DEC. 22. 1937	DEC. 29. 1937	JAN. 5. 1938	JAN. 12. 1938
JAN. 26. 1938	FEB. 2. 1938	FEB. 9. 1938	FEB. 16. 1938	FEB. 23. 1938	MAR. 2. 1938	MAR. 9. 1938	MAR. 16. 1938	MAR. 23. 1938	MAR. 30. 1938	APRIL 6. 1938	APRIL 13. 1938	APRIL 20. 1938	APRIL 27. 1938
MAY 11. 1938	MAY 18. 1938	MAY 25. 1938	JUNE 1. 1938	JUNE 8. 1938	JUNE 15. 1938	JUNE 22. 1938	JUNE 29. 1938	JULY 6. 1938	JULY 13. 1938	JULY 20. 1938	JULY 27. 1938	AUG. 3. 1938	

Left, Anita, R. J. and Bill Bennett in 1937. Just before this picture was taken, Bill had been playing with a pair of shears and had cut his own hair. It is shorter than he usually wore it.

Below, Bill Bennett, in a family snapshot, in the early 1940s.

W.A.C. Bennett in full Masonic regalia in 1945.

Cecil and May Bennett on their 25th wedding anniversary.

The British Columbia Social Credit League convention in Vancouver, in 1953. W.A.C. Bennett and Alberta Premier Ernest Manning are shown in the insert at lower right.

sidelines, hugged himself with glee as the lethargic Johnson was forced to lumber into action against his headline-stealing finance minister. Anscomb's resignation was asked for and received, but three other Conservative members in the coalition went with him; shortly after, eleven more Conservatives followed suit.

Johnson and his Liberals were now alone. Everybody waited for him to call the inevitable election. But he procrastinated. This allowed Anscomb to play whatever role suited his Conservatives best. On one day he could be the official opposition and on the next prop up Johnson's tottering government. But Anscomb's manipulations, no less than Johnson's inertia, played into the hands of the Socreds and the CCF. "This is what the old parties have led us to," they said, "a caretaker in office and a clown leading the opposition."

The charade lasted five weeks; then Johnson capitulated under pressure from his advisors. He dissolved the government and called an election. On June 12, 1952, British Columbia voters had to decide on the question of the sale of liquor by the glass, the adoption of daylight-saving time and whether or not they wanted a new kind of government.

IF WE WERE to become even a minority government, I had to use clear-cut strategy in that first election of 1952. I had to proceed point by point and area by area. I always say, there are no patent-medicine kind of solutions because every voter is an individual.

First I had to fight for the Socred nomination in my own riding, because they had put up somebody else to run against me. I won that nomination. But I was not party leader. We had only appointed a campaign manager, because we wanted to make sure that we had a leader with a seat in the legislature.

During the campaign I drove day and night around the province, sleeping many times in my car and living out of a suitcase. I'd drop in at my home just for a change of linens. After all, it was no use for me to stay around the Okanagan Valley and Kelowna, when I knew I'd be elected anyway. I campaigned elsewhere so I wouldn't be just one single member sitting in Victoria. I helped out candidates everywhere.

I got many telegrams from my new Socred friends in Kelowna and the South Okanagan. Although they hardly knew me, they asked me to come home. "They are saying terrible things about you, please come home, it's awful." I just threw these telegrams in the wastepaper basket; I didn't even bother to tear them up.

One week before the election, I was in Golden speaking for Orr Newton, who'd never made a political speech before. We had a tremendous meeting there and we won that seat. The Kelowna Socreds sent me another telegram, "Don't come home, all is lost, all is lost, don't come home. Withdraw instead." My enemies and the press were saying, "The reason why Bennett is not campaigning in Kelowna and South Okanagan is that he's afraid to face the music; he knows very well he's not going to get elected in his own riding, so that's why he's not showing his face."

After I had received that telegram, I phoned the only movie theatre in Kelowna and asked the owner to put up a great big sign, "Bennett Answers the Political Machines: Saturday, Doors Open at Six. All Welcome!" In addition I ordered ten spot announcements a day to run on one radio station for that entire week. And in the newspapers we had the same thing—"Bennett Answers the Political Machines!"

Herbert Anscomb, vindictive to the end, organized a meeting in Kelowna for the same evening. He wanted to wreck mine. As the Conservatives were assembling in Scout Hall, I sent a scout to their gathering. Apart from entertainers and speakers, I found out that they had an audience of five. In front of the theatre where my meeting was to be held it was jammed and people were lined up three blocks up the street. Not everybody could get in and we had to hold the meeting twice.

But still my friends were telling me, "We supported you when you ran federally, we supported you as a Conservative and a coalitionist. But if you are going to represent that funny money, Bible-punching party, we're not going to support you any longer. You haven't got a chance, Bennett. Your old party has a chance. They've got the mayor of Kelowna running and not a single Conservative will be voting for you. And the

Liberals have that fine chap, Captain Cecil Bull, that used to be the MLA before you came; he'll take all the Liberal votes. And the socialist votes are CCF votes. Now where is there room for you?"

There didn't seem to be any room for me. I had not one vote from my friends, the business fraternity on the main streets. I had not even one vote among the professional groups, the doctors, the lawyers, the chartered accountants. But it wasn't just these groups that voted in that election, others came from everywhere to vote.

I was walking down the street to the theatre on the night of the meeting when a fellow came up to me, hit me on the shoulder and asked, "Your name Bennett?"

"Yes, my name's Bennett," I replied.

"Me Social Credit too," he said. The man was a sheep herder from the hills who'd never voted in his life before. Yes, they came from everywhere to vote in that election.

People wanted change, people wanted action. They were tired of promises, promises, promises, tired of having to put up with a terrible highway system and a government that would bring out the yellow road machinery one week before the election and take it back to the yards one day after the election. That's why people were saying, "Here's this chap Bennett; he's fifty-one years old, he's never promised us any special deals. He says he's going to do things. Let's give him a chance, let's follow him."

Travelling salesmen would come into the store and ask, "How is Social Credit going, W. A. C.?"

I'd say, "Just going like wildfire." Then they'd go on to Vernon and ask, "How's Social Credit, up here?"

"We've never heard of it," they'd say.

"Oh. Down in Kelowna, it's going like wildfire," the travellers would tell them.

They were the people who spread the message. All advertising is good, wonderful, powerful, but when the message is spread by word of mouth, it's the very best kind. We had it going all over the province. You could just feel it in the air.

Only the press couldn't feel it. Hornets meet hornets, flies meet flies, birds of a feather flock together, and the same goes for newsmen. They meet at the Press Club, for lunch, all talking the same stuff. They start to believe their own propaganda. Most of them can't run and get themselves elected, but they don't mind standing above the government telling the government what to do, as long as they don't have to be on the firing line. If you want to be in politics you have to be on the firing line. Politics, to me, is the most interesting and the most vital profession. People should be in public life, just for the fun of it. Of course, if a person has nothing to contribute and doesn't have a burning desire to do something, he should stay out of public life. He should be a lawyer, a hardware merchant, or perhaps an interviewer. But if a person is young and wants to do something he considers worthwhile, he should be encouraged to get into public life as soon as he's in proper financial shape.

In 1952, we voted by transferable ballot. For example, if four candidates were running in your riding, you could vote for your first, second and third choices. On the first count, only first choices were counted. If one person got an overall majority—more than half the votes—he was automatically elected, and the other votes were never counted. But if he didn't get an overall majority, the second choices on the other three candidates' ballots were counted. Then, if someone had an overall majority, the counting stopped. If none of the candidates had an overall majority, they counted the third choices on the other two. By that time, someone was bound to have an overall majority. It was a very simple system. I had convinced the Conservatives and Liberals to introduce the transferable ballot. They needed something like that to prevent the breakup of the coalition.

When the votes were counted in Kelowna on election night, I had received more than all the other three parties put together. I was elected on the first count, as were three other Social Crediters. But we didn't find out until July that we were going to have nineteen seats in the legislature. The CCF had eighteen. Our nineteenth member was Cyril Shelford, the farmer from Kitimat.

6

An Impossible Job

The 1952 elections were over. The lengthy process of recounts began. It was nerve-wracking: the first count yielded only four MLAs clearly enough in the lead to be declared elected. All four were Social Crediters.

The next day, the flustered returning officers could only give approximate results: besides the four elected, Social Credit was leading in ten, but the CCF was leading in twenty-one.

At the beginning of July, almost a month after the election, all that was certain was that Social Credit and the CCF were tied with fourteen seats apiece, Social Credit leading in three, the CCF in two.

As nominal leader of the party with the most seats, W. A. C. Bennett was floundering in a sea of advice. Voices all around him urged a coalition. After more than a decade of joint-party rule, British Columbians were fixed in the glue of coalition. Bennett listened, smiled enigmatically as he thanked everyone and kept his own counsel.

For one thing, he was not the leader of the party yet, only the man who had engineered the victory. The Reverend Hansell still lurked in the background, ever hopeful of the leadership the Albertan hierarchy had said was his. He joined forces with a tough old Scottish MLA from Delta, Thomas J. Irwin, in a conspiracy to push Bennett out. Hansell did not qualify to hold office in British Columbia, because he had not lived there for one year. Irwin had been a resident for years. They planned to get him elected as leader, put Hansell in as his executive assistant and then switch positions when Hansell had been in British Columbia for one year.

W. A. C. Bennett paid not the slightest attention to them. He had bigger things on his mind, such as forming a cabinet.

Two men were essential to him, and they would have to be brought in from the outside. They were Robert Bonner and Einar Gunderson.

Bonner had become a war hero at the age of twenty-one, serving with the Seaforths in Africa, Sicily and Italy during the Second World War. Invalided out with head injuries and the rank of lieutenant-colonel—a spectacular achievement for one so young—he had taken a law degree at the University of British Columbia and then joined Conservative politics as a cool and urbane opponent of the blustery Herbert Anscomb. Bennett made Bonner attorney-general.

Einar Gunderson, the second man, received the finance portfolio. A massive-framed man with a ponderous though jovial manner, Gunderson had been born in Copperston, North Dakota to Icelandic parents. Having taken his chartered accountant's degree at the University of Saskatchewan, he had made a name for himself in Alberta's civil service under the United Farmers' government. In private practice until 1935, he then joined Marshall Wells, where he rose to the position of comptroller in 1942. He stayed with the company's Canadian subsidiary until the war's end, when he came to Vancouver to become a partner in Gunderson, Stokes, Peers, Walton and Company, the firm that handled the accounting for Bennett's burgeoning hardware chain. Gunderson had ties with Ottawa through his post as chairman of the taxation committees of the Vancouver Board of Trade and the Institute of Chartered Accountants of British Columbia.

W. A. C. Bennett worked quietly away, his goals firmly fixed in his mind.

I STARTED TO FORM my government, even though I had not yet been chosen party leader. I knew it was an impossible job to actively seek the leadership, as it was the kind of job you'd accept only if your peers especially wanted you. It had all happened in such a short time that I had not had an opportunity to meet many of the members we had elected to assess their backgrounds.

We held a meeting at the Hotel Vancouver, which included our defeated Socred candidates although they could not vote. Four men were running for leadership. There was

Tom Irwin, who later became Speaker of the House, and
Philip Gaglardi, whom I made minister of public works.
There was Peer Paynter, a party organizer who wasn't even a
member-elect, and I. They all made their speeches, saying that
Social Credit had all the answers, that they could easily handle
the job, and knew just how to do it. Some of them hadn't ever
seen the parliament buildings before, but that didn't seem to
make any difference to them. They still believed they could do
the job. That was their opinion, and they were entitled to it. I
was the last one to speak.

I had met T. D. Pattullo, the Liberal premier between 1933
and 1941 who, when re-elected in a minority government with
twenty-one members, not with nineteen as we had been elected,
had been forced by his party to accept a coalition with the
Conservatives. Pattullo then left the Liberals and sat in the
House as an independent member.

The Liberals under Pattullo had been experienced parlia-
mentarians; we were not. I knew that whoever assumed the
task of leading this minority group would have a difficult job.

We were under pressure to establish medicare. The people
expected it and I wanted it for them. We needed to advance on
the educational front; new schools had to be built. We had
campaigned with a new school formula, to support operations
and initiate a capital building program. The schools were
owned by local school boards, not by the provincial government. There had to be a proper financial formula. We only
had one small university, the University of British Columbia;
it had to be enlarged and made into a great learning institution.
And we'd need two more. Later, we built Simon Fraser in
Greater Vancouver and also added the University of Victoria.
The original crown colony of Vancouver Island was entitled
to have a seat of higher learning and we'd have to see to it that
it got one. This and so much more had to be done. The province was in a turmoil, and there were strikes everywhere. We
needed to build highways, proper bridges, tunnels and ferries.
Power had to be developed for new industries which, in turn,
could create new jobs. The provincial debt had to be paid off

first so that we could finance all these projects later. We had to pay off that debt and create surpluses at the same time.

This was an impossible task for any one person; and I knew it. That was why I told the delegates that I didn't think I could do the job. I was honest when I rejected the leadership ... but history has proved me wrong.

When the vote was taken by secret ballot, two of the other three candidates each received one vote, one man got two votes and I received the rest. The returning officer looked at us and said, "What shall I do with the ballots which have been designated for the second, third and fourth balloting?"

Someone called out to him, "You foolish fellow, the darn thing's over. Declare the man with the all-round majority elected!" That man was me. It all happened inside of five or ten minutes. There was great excitement. The press were waiting, and the people had assembled outside knowing that the Socreds would choose a leader to be the next premier of British Columbia.

I told the delegates that we would do more than just step outside and make the announcement; I suggested that, "as we've got some work to do anyway, before we meet the public or the press, I would like every elected member to speak for five or ten minutes."

Now, I had my opportunity to size up each one of my people. I was their leader. I even asked those who had been defeated to make a short speech, to see what kind of talent we could count on for the next election. With a minority government, I knew we would have to go to the polls again within the next twelve months.

Forty-seven people ended up making speeches, and the press and everybody else were getting very impatient. They said, "They must be having an awful fight in there." They would never believe that there was no fight at all.

When I got back to Kelowna, I telegraphed Robert Bonner and Einar Gunderson to get the news to them quickly. Although they had their offices in the same building in Vancouver, they did not know each other. My telegram to each of them read, "Please meet me at eight o'clock tomorrow night in the dining room of Pinewoods Lodge at the top of the Hope Highway." Neither of them knew that the other was receiving the message.

I was a few minutes early getting to the lodge. I reserved a table for the three of us, and when they arrived, I had dinner with both of them. They were very surprised to see each other. Right in front of Gunderson, I told Bonner that when I became premier, I wanted him to be my attorney-general, and I said to Gunderson, in front of Bonner, "and I want you to be my finance minister."

At first they were hesitant to accept my offer, as neither of them had much confidence in Social Credit as such, especially not in Social Credit MLAs. But both felt better for seeing each other there; Einar Gunderson, a strong Liberal, had set up the tax department for the Alberta government before Social Credit came to power. I remember how I had dropped in to see him one day and noticed a picture of the former premier of Alberta on the wall of his office. I said, "Don't worry, you don't have to turn his face to the wall."

Now, sitting at the dinner table, I said, "Mr. Gunderson, I want sound finance, balanced budgets, and dynamic policies." And then addressing Bonner, the Conservative federal representative in British Columbia, I said, "As attorney-general, you must operate your department without political patronage. There has been a lot of that in the past."

Then one of them interjected, "How do we get seats in the legislature, Mr. Bennett? We haven't been elected."

"That's my responsibility," I told them. "I would not ask you to do something that I haven't thought out beforehand. You trust me, don't you? You trust my judgment in having selected you? Now you must trust my judgment further and believe me when I tell you that I have a plan."

"Tell us about it! We can keep a secret," they said.

"I can keep a secret too," I replied. "When more than one person has a secret, there is no secret." We shook hands and I went back to Kelowna.

In July, about six weeks after the election, I started to plan how and where my nineteen MLAs could make the best contribution to the welfare of the people of British Columbia. I worked quietly on that project and took no one into my confidence.

Bjorn Johnson had been defeated and Herbert Anscomb was also out of the race; yet the lieutenant-governor had not taken steps toward asking anybody else to form a new government. Both Bennett and Harold Winch were waiting to see the last recount from Burrard Riding, and Winch entertained hopes that the recount would bring him victory. Failing that, he looked to Tom Uphill, the staunch Labour independent, to support him and his kissing cousins in the CCF.

But Cecil Bennett and Tom Uphill had been great friends from the very first day of Bennett's parliamentary career. One day in the House, Uphill had sent him a note which read, "Dear Cece, will you please make a donation to the Labour Party?" Bennett had sent back a note, "Dear Tom, here's a five dollar bill. Who or what is the Labour Party?" Back came the reply: "My very, very good friend Cece. I am the Labour Party and I'll drink your health on it tonight."

Now, in 1952, Cece Bennett had another note from his old friend Tom, which said that the Labour Party wished him the best of luck and was hoping that he would be the one to form the next government. It was a letter Bennett would keep in his pocket for future eventualities.

FINALLY, ALL THE RECOUNTING was over. Without doubt, we were nineteen. The CCF had eighteen members and Tom Uphill had won one seat to represent the Labour Party. Then the cry went up all over British Columbia, "The lieutenant-governor must call on W. A. C. Bennett to form the next government."

Even Percy Richards, the executive assistant to the premier, telephoned me in Kelowna. "I want you to know, Mr. Bennett, that the government's going to recommend you to the lieutenant-governor."

I thanked him for his confidence. Then he wanted to know if he could be my executive assistant. "No, Mr. Richards," I told him, "this is a brand-new ball game."

Next I sent telegrams to all those I wanted in my first cabinet, asking them to meet me in Victoria. I would stay at the Empress Hotel, and I didn't want any of them staying at the same place. I had cautioned them not to reveal to any other MLAs why they were in the capital. "There is no air of mystery about this, so just act naturally," I said.

When all of us had arrived in Victoria, I phoned each one of them to chat casually, and in the course of our conversations I mentioned to them for the very first time why they were there. "I want you in my cabinet; but you are not to tell anybody about it, not even your own wives." I would tell them later what portfolios they would have, cautioning them to take it easy meantime, and to enjoy the lovely weather. It was beautiful in Victoria at the end of July 1952, just beautiful, warm and beautiful.

Now it was time to make an appointment with Tilly Rolston, who was one of my MLAs-elect. We met in the rotunda of the Empress Hotel the next morning, planning to have breakfast together, but knowing full well that, as soon as we would enter the dining room, the messages would fly. Pretty soon reporters were all around us. "Why are you and Mrs. Rolston sitting together in the dining room of the Empress Hotel?" they wanted to know.

"Why," I said, "who wouldn't want to come to Victoria at this time of the year? It's beautiful weather, the scenery is beautiful, and everything is wonderful."

"Are you here for other reasons?"

"Certainly, lots of reasons."

"Are you here to form the new government?"

"What new government?" I replied.

They went away and I was glad, because I needed that message to reach the legislative buildings immediately so that the premier and his cabinet would call a meeting. They did, and announced that they were going to resign.

Bob Bonner was in my suite with me. He asked, "When will you be called?"

"Before the day is out," I said. This was August 1.

"Have you had word from the lieutenant-governor?"

"No. But the phone will ring, Bonner; don't worry."

The phone did ring. It was the lieutenant-governor's aide and then Clarence Wallace himself came on the line. Could I come to see him? It was nothing important, but he was taking the CPR boat to Vancouver that night, headed for the Okanagan Valley, he thought he would just like to have a chat with me before he left. We arranged to meet.

Ronald Worley, the chap who later became my executive assistant, had an old car, parked two or three blocks away. He walked one way and I went another. Nobody saw us leave together. We met and drove off, pretending to make a couple of calls on the way to throw everybody off just in case someone had been watching us. Of course, they were on our trail, but they lost us before we headed for Government House.

Ronald Worley had to remain outside, of course, and Mr. Wallace and I had tea in his study. We chatted, and he told me about his trips to the interior. I told him what dire straits British Columbia was in and had been for some time. Never before had there been a similar situation in the province. Since the election, between June 12 and August 1, no effective government had been in power. Chaos was rampant. Labour and management and everything else were in a turmoil. Something had to be done right away, right away. "We must have a government," I said, "like tonight, Your Honour!"

That shook him. "Ah, well," he said, "I hadn't thought of that."

"Your Honour, my new cabinet is in Victoria, in your capital, it is ready to be sworn in. All the papers have been drawn up with the exception of the portfolios, which I shall insert at the last minute. My ministers-elect can be here in half an hour."

Somewhat taken aback, he replied with caution, "Ah, I don't think I can do that. I'm getting different advice. I'm sure I can't do that." And, "Ah, it was a very close race between you and the CCF. And they've got a Labour member, Mr. Tom Uphill, to support them. That gives them nineteen members. And they've got the longest experience in the House, your people haven't. They were the official opposition, they've been there for a long time. Some of my advisors think they should be called. And they have told me not to do anything right now."

Gordon Sloan, chief justice of the province, was a wonderful man, a very astute person who had been attorney-general for many years under a Liberal government. He had undertaken exhaustive studies of our forest industry. Apparently, it was he who had recommended to the lieutenant-governor that we not be called.

"Well Your Honour," I replied, "remember, I was elected on the first ballot on June 12, and so were some of those who will be my MLAs. The people of this province have been very patient during this difficult period, and I've been patient, too. I must inform you, Your Honour, with all due deference but in all seriousness, that unless our government is sworn in this night before you leave for the interior, we shall be in touch with the news media, the radio and the others. You know that the people of this province expect the Social Credit Party, the party I lead, to be called to form the next government. You mentioned Mr. Tom Uphill, the Labour member from Fernie; are you telling me that he will make up the nineteenth member for the CCF? I have a letter from Mr. Uphill·in my pocket, congratulating me on my victory and saying that he knows full well that we'll be called upon to be the next government."

I had been forthright and firm. Now I became very quiet. The lieutenant-governor could see the situation he was in. But being a great British-Columbian Canadian, he also realized that the province was in an intolerable situation and that he had to restore confidence.

I went on, "The people are watching us today. Let us not create further chaos. Let us be part of the solution, instead of part of the problem. You say you have to take the midnight boat? Very well, then we can be sworn in before this evening. We're ready, we're prepared." I looked at the time; it was about four o'clock in the afternoon.

"So you have all the papers?" he asked.

"Yes."

"Who has prepared them?"

"Captain Pennington, the deputy provincial secretary."

"Does he know you're here?"

"No. Nobody knows but you and I, and Mr. Robert Bonner, who happened to be in my hotel suite when you called."

Lieutenant-governor Clarence Wallace looked terribly worried. "Well, Mr. Bennett," he said, "I've got to think this over quietly." I knew he wanted to talk to Chief Justice Sloan again and to his other advisors. He repeated, "I've got to think this over quietly, but I'll phone you later this afternoon."

I thanked him and left Government House. When I got into the car, Worley asked me, "Are we the government?"

I said, "What government? We just had a friendly call."

When we got back to the Empress Hotel, Bonner was pacing the floor. In his hand he had a copy of the Victoria *Times*, a newspaper that has generally been wrong through the years. It carried a story stating that Social Credit would not be called to form the next government.

Pointing to the article, Bonner said, "Well, I guess I'll go back to my law office in Vancouver."

"Mr. Bonner," I replied, "this is your first lesson in real politics. The apparent is often not the real situation. Before this night's out you'll be sworn in as the youngest, most brilliant attorney-general our province has ever seen."

He just laughed. "Oh," he said, "you're amazing."

We waited for the phone to ring, but the phone didn't ring. The phone didn't ring. The phone didn't ring. The phone didn't ring. Then, it rang!

It was the lieutenant-governor. "Mr. Bennett," he said,

"when did you say you could come to be sworn in?"

"Any time, Your Honour, any time."

"Would nine o'clock tonight be satisfactory, *Mr. Premier?*"

"We'll be there, Your Honour, we'll be there."

"I'm only sorry I can't arrange a little dinner for the new government. But we'll have some sandwiches here."

"That's immaterial, Your Honour. I know you're packed to leave for Vancouver. We'll be there."

I called Ronald Worley and told him to contact all the chaps who would be in the cabinet. "Get in touch with them, no matter what you have to do. Get in touch with the press gallery; tell them to come, we'll have sandwiches for them. In the meantime, Worley, get the papers ready for the swearing in of the ministers. Fill them in. These are the portfolios each will receive; I'll be president of the Executive Council of course, Gunderson will be finance minister, Bonner, attorney-general, and so forth." That was the first time Worley heard the news.

Elated, they all assembled. Everybody was floating on the ceiling, asking the others about their portfolios. "What have you got, what have you got there?" Most of them were such novices they hardly knew what a provincial secretary was. We drove out to Government House in taxis. As none of them could even tell their wives why they were in Victoria, each one had to go alone.

When we arrived at Government House, the press was already there. As part of the welcoming committee, I was pleased to see Chief Justice Sloan. Then we were all sworn and everything went well. We hustled away, so that His Honour could catch the midnight boat to Vancouver.

Back at the Empress Hotel, we called for room service. Because of the excitement nobody had eaten much lunch. When the waitress asked what they'd have to drink, Gunderson, I think, said, "Make mine a whiskey and soda."

The waitress replied, "Mr. Gunderson, I'm sorry, that's not the choice."

"What is the choice?" he asked.

"Tea, coffee or Ovaltine."

"Then make mine Ovaltine," said Gunderson.

We all had Ovaltine. It was a good party and I believe ours was the first government ever to be sworn in and toasted with Ovaltine.

7

A Leisurely Stroll

The fledgling ministers assembled in the salon of the Empress Hotel did not present the most reassuring sight to the new premier. Bennett knew that some of them had had to ask directions to find the hotel, and many would take days to discover where their offices were located. The situation called for strong doses of optimism, pluck and positive cheerfulness—qualities Bennett had imbibed from the books of Dr. Orison Swett Marsden. The good doctor, incidentally, had also prescribed Ovaltine as an essential ingredient of success for the man who would rise above the modesty of his means.

Now, as the steaming wholesome brew was quaffed by those who were used to stronger stuff, Bennett tried to judge how well they would do in the spots he had assigned to them. There was the Reverend Philip Gaglardi, a man of diverse talents. One of a family of twelve children, he had helped to support them by working first as a grocery-store attendant and then as a harvest-machinery mechanic. Next, he had graduated to road construction, as a labourer, at first, then as a general driver and finally as a bulldozer operator. He knew the underside of the work force that a minister of public works would have to administrate.

Then there was Robert Sommers, listed as a school principal but better known as a man with a penchant for putting out forest fires in the Castlegar district. He was also a Kiwanian and an accomplished trumpet and poker player, and now he was minister of lands, forests and mines.

Kenneth Kiernan, who had received the agriculture portfolio, had one advantage over many of his fellow ministers. Having been reared in Victoria, he did know the way to his own front door. So did Tilly Rolston, a teacher for two years before she was married in 1909. As a grandmother of nine, she was now Bennett's minister of education. Lyle Wicks, the one-time motorman, was minister of labour. Eric Martin, an accountant who had ridden the rails during the Depression, later serving as a physical education instructor in the Canadian Army, held the contentious health and welfare post. Only he and Tilly Rolston had some administrative and political experience. Martin had run four times as a Socred and had served as the party's vice-president in 1945 and 1951.

The Honourable W. R. T. Chetwynd was minister of trade, industry and railways. He had come from Litchfield in Staffordshire, taken a degree in agriculture at Pullman State College in Washington, and worked ten years as a public relations man for the Pacific Great Eastern. After that he had become a rancher and later served as director of the British Columbia Livestock Exchange. During that time he had written a play called *Heifer Dust Inn*, a fact that happily remained unknown to the general public and to W. A. C. Bennett.

Finally he had Bonner and Gunderson, major pillars of support for Bennett, who would train, cajole and hold together the rest of this group of inexperienced ministers.

THE NEXT DAY was August 2. We met in my suite at the Empress Hotel in Victoria, and as the legislative building is just a short walk from there, we didn't have to get cabs or drive cars—but could just walk across. So my ministers and I walked over together. Of course, the press described it as a "march," but it was nothing more than a leisurely stroll.

We were met by Percy Richards, the executive assistant to Premier Johnson. He had a statement prepared for me to read. It contained a lot of propaganda for the old parties and stuff to that effect. Of course, I set it aside. I made my own statement, thanking the previous government and wishing the ex-premier well.

Later, Percy Richards asked me for a recommendation, which I agreed to write as I'd known him for a long time and considered him a good and honest person. Instead of drafting

the letter myself, I told him to dictate his own recommendation, and "I shall sign it," I said. I knew he wouldn't put anything there that was more than the truth. You see, when you
put a person on his mettle, you bring out the best in him.

I sat in the office for the first time as premier. That's
when I told my ministers, "You'll have a lot of problems, and
so will I. Don't bring your problems to me, because for every
one you have I've got a dozen. Go back and learn the workings
of your departments; get to know them better than your deputy
ministers. But when you come to some problem that you really
can't solve, I don't want you to come with just the problem. I
want you to come with the solution to the problem, with at
least three different alternatives. Be willing and able to argue
in favour of all three, the pros and cons. And then, if you want
my help, I'll help you make the decision. I'll help you make
the decision, which is the right choice."

The system worked well. Sometimes a cabinet minister
would come to me and say, "Mr. Premier, I've got six problems."

"That's fine," I would say, "write them down, write them
down."

Then I would ask him for a piece of paper to put across
his list in such a way that I could see only the top problem. I'd
read the first one and ask him how he would solve it. He
would make a suggestion. He'd have given it a lot of thought.
Then I would tick off number one and go on to the next, taking the six problems one by one. That would take no more
than a few minutes.

That is how I tried to teach them. "If you have six or
seven problems on your mind all at once, then you are not
thinking, you are worrying. But if you write them down one
by one and concentrate on them one at a time, the solutions
will come easily. I'm a hardware merchant," I would say. "We
sell rope, thick rope that you cannot break. But if you take
each strand separately, you can break the rope in a few
minutes."

Government and business are simple. It's only people
who make them complicated. They call a conference for this,

and another one for that. They write memos to cover up what they do not know. As a rule, the bigger the business or the government, the less efficient it will be.

A good salesman is not a person who says, "I'm a good salesman." In fact, a good salesman is never a salesman at all, but a person who creates in the minds of others the want for this or that kind of policy, merchandise or service. He must stimulate in others the desire to buy his ideas or his goods. A good salesman knows what he's doing, just as a good minister knows the policy of his government. Only then can he have an objective and go straight ahead to accomplish his task.

On the first day, I said to my cabinet, "I want you to be busy, but I don't want you to be busy cross-piling sawdust, the way they do in Ottawa. I don't want to see your desks cluttered with papers, and you telling me how you're working yourselves to death. If you can't get your work done by five o'clock in the evening, there's something wrong. Your mind isn't organized."

My ministers knew how everybody was watching our performance. They realized that they could not get away with the things the old governments had gotten away with. We had no supporters among the press or the media, and my activities and movements were being observed day and night; everyone knew what time I went home and who I was with.

One day a Liberal friend said to me, "Our party has had a detective following you night and day. Here's what he wrote about you:

"'He lives a more quiet life than a Baptist minister.'"

Mrs. Bennett and I had rented an apartment on Oak Bay in Victoria, a small beautiful place overlooking the water; certainly adequate for the two of us. We bought it many years later and lived in it for twenty years.

I could live the way I knew I wanted to live, but I could not dictate to my ministers what kind of lives they should lead. Yet, I had to tell them not to have a bunch of liquor cabinets in their offices in the parliament buildings. "I want them all taken out within half an hour," I said. Some of the wives had been complaining that from time to time their husbands had arrived home under the influence of liquor, and their children had seen them in that condition. These women knew that liquor could be obtained from the government. When I became premier of the province, I was determined to stop the practice. I didn't stop people from having parties, but my rule was: no liquor of any kind inside the parliament buildings.

I also warned each man in my cabinet not to go out at night with a lady, unless she was his wife. "You're going to be watched, and watched, and watched, so make sure you walk under the lights where everybody can see that the lady you're with is your wife."

Everybody wrote us off, right from the start, and not even the Socreds thought the new government would last longer than a week.

But our priorities had been established earlier. We knew we had to get British Columbia moving again, and solve the problems despite the fact that we were in the minority. I was determined to proceed as though we were a majority government and thought that the combined opposition would at first be afraid to call another election. I hoped that they would support us and we could boldly go ahead with our program.

So we went right ahead and cancelled all the special lists that had been kept in the Department of Highways and used for the bidding on highway construction. Now everybody could bid, and the lowest bidder got the contract. These directives were also applicable to public works and we advised the Purchasing Commission to destroy or burn their special patronage file listing dealers throughout the province. Everybody had a right to tender. The Purchasing Commission realized that we meant business and that if they refused to carry out our policy their jobs would be on the line. In the end, I think they even welcomed those guidelines.

We called for tenders to purchase cars for the departments, to replace some of the old ones. We did not get a special price. But I knew the federal government was getting a 3 percent quantity discount and I asked, "Why shouldn't we?"

I was told there were no discounts on cars or trucks for the provincial government. So we didn't buy any until we had assembled a large quantity of orders, over a period of time. Then we let different companies bid. We knew that would tempt them to cut prices. The old government had paid full retail prices for their purchases. We saved millions of dollars, under Social Credit's dynamic competitive system, receiving discounts of up to 20 percent.

Paints, oil, and other supplies were purchased at prices lower than those paid in other parts of Canada. Businesses knew that if they offered us a good deal they would get the orders. I told all the suppliers, "Social Credit will give away only one thing—if you don't already have one—a pencil sharpener to sharpen your pencils, so that we can get better prices."

I warned my ministers that, during the time they were in the service of the government, they could not benefit personally from their positions of trust. One of them said to me, "Don't worry, Mr. Premier; I'll treat the government's monies just like my own."

"Oh, no, you won't," I said, "not as long as I'm premier. That money is tax money, it's trust money, and I want one hundred and ten cents worth of value out of every dollar. Remember that."

Once again, the luck that had been with Bennett in Edmonton and Kelowna held. The exchequer he inherited was bulging with the fruits of delirious growth in the private sector. Alcan's $100 million project in Kitimat was nearing completion just as Shell Oil was paying out $50 million for additional refinery facilities in Burnaby. Over the mountains, a pipeline snaked its way through to deliver 125,000 barrels of Alberta oil a day to that same refinery. Pipelines to carry British Columbia and Alberta natural gas to Vancouver and the coast cities were on the drawing boards.

The forestry industry was booming—perhaps not as economic nationalists might have liked, as a few massive conglomerates controlled the millions of linear feet of lumber that went mainly to the United States. Nearly all the saws that howled in the forests belonged to MacMillan Bloedel, B.C. Forest Products, Alaska Pine and a handful of others. What the saws felled, other giants pulped. The Columbia Cellulose Company, an American subsidiary of the Celanese Corporation, sent 900,000 tons of forest products southward each year.

Towns that had stagnated for decades now leapt to life. Prince George, Quesnel, Hazleton and Castlegar spawned new suburbs and new industries. In the Nechako and Prince Rupert Districts, new sawmills sprang up, trees began to fall beyond the Peace River and in the forests between Dawson Creek and White River.

The Liberals knew to the last penny how much they had left behind in the treasury till. They also knew how many municipal demands were going to be made on that surplus. Everyone wanted services after so many years of stagnation and neglect. The Liberals waited gleefully for Bennett to make a wrong move; then they would leap back into power.

Bennett would have to act with great caution. First, he had to find safe seats for Gunderson and Bonner, the only two professionals in his cabinet. Neither could sit in the House without being elected, although exceptions had been made in the past, sometimes due to wartime emergencies. As this was peacetime, Bennett was forced to bump two of his elected members from their ridings, a move which under previous administrations would have meant a fat reward for the bumped member.

M̲R. BONNER AND MR. GUNDERSON now were full-fledged cabinet ministers, having been sworn in by the lieutenant-governor. They had taken their oaths of office in accordance with the British parliamentary system. But, although proper procedure had been followed, these ministers could not sit in the legislature without a seat.

Vancouver Island had no Social Credit representation in the House. Therefore, the island had no cabinet representation. I asked publicly for two of the Conservatives or Liberals to resign their seats, to allow my ministers to run. Of course, they refused.

Then the clever press corps went to all my MLAs and

asked them if they were going to resign to make room for the two cabinet ministers Bennett had appointed. "Are you going to give up your seat for them?" they asked.

"No way!" they said. "We have been elected by our people; we're their MLAs."

Then I talked to my MLAs. I was forthright and told them that if they were genuine Social Crediters who believed in the future of our party and in our present government, they surely would, if they had a chance, assist in making it work. "We need a lawyer as attorney-general on our side of the House and we've got the best in Bonner," I told them. "We need Gunderson as our finance minister. I cannot appeal to you if your personal ambition is so close to your eyes that you cannot see anything else. But if you're not out just for yourself, then resign your seat and let these men run in by-elections."

I was willing to give them a commitment, if they vacated these seats, that Bonner and Gunderson would not run in the next general election, which I was sure would come within a year. "It's only for a year," I said. "If your ridings want you then and you are ready to be nominated, you will be candidates the second time round. In the next election, these ministers will have to run in other ridings."

I talked to quite a number, and I got two of my members to resign their seats. We had formed a government on August 1, 1952 and the by-elections were held in November of that same year. Gunderson ran in Similkameen riding, in the Okanagan Valley, Bonner in Columbia, in the Columbia River Valley. Both men were elected with big majorities. If we had lost either of these by-elections, we would have lost our plurality in the House; and if we had lost both, we certainly would have been out.

Both by-elections had moments of comedy. Gunderson had to placate the irate voters of Similkameen by contradicting earlier statements by health and welfare minister Eric Martin. The latter had said that the United Nations was the most dangerous phenomenon of modern times. Although most of the voters probably agreed with him under their breath, United Nations troops—including Canadians—were at that moment fighting in Korea. In principle, these voters felt, it was in bad form to criticize an organization that was engaged in killing Communists.

Bonner left his panelled Vancouver offices to walk gingerly along the tree-lined dirt roads of the Columbia riding. At one meeting, he promised the voters cheaper long-distance telephone rates. Unfortunately, only one resident of the area had a telephone and that was hand-cranked. The other people in the neighbourhood were afraid to use it because they said it gave them electric shocks.

By the time Bonner and Gunderson finally joined Bennett in the House, he had taken firm control of the party, structurally and financially. John Perdue, Kenneth Kiernan's organizer, had won the party presidency from Shantz and Paynter, and was now Bennett's man. The Alberta oil money that had funded internal opposition to Bennett came under his control when he ordered the party's various fund-raising groups to report directly to Gunderson's accounting firm. In this way Bennett knew exactly where every penny in the party war chest had been raised and how it was being spent.

In the House Bennett set the style and the others followed. Most of the members were awed to sit in the same chambers where McBride had roistered and Pattullo had schemed. So much did they look to Bennett for guidance that when he chattered, they did as well, and when he fired off a retort, they followed suit. Their benches were so noisy that one disgruntled Liberal asked the Speaker to chide them for "simian behaviour." During the first Throne Speech debate, which lasted ten days, they remained silent at Bennett's request because, as he told them, "I wish to move on quickly to discuss the budget Gunderson has prepared." Their silence led to grumbling among the opposition, which accused the Socred MLAs of being "deaf and dumb tailors' dummies, controlled by Bennett in his ivory tower."

When Gunderson presented his budget, he cut $5.5 million from government expenditures, lowered the cost of auto licenses, raised the exemption on the tax on restaurant meals, and imposed a new 10 percent tax on the huge resource companies. The men from MacMillan Bloedel and the big mining companies winced in the gallery as the tax was announced. Their minions would raise a wave of indignation in the British Columbia Manufacturer's Association and in the Association of British Columbia Loggers, but the tax would remain.

If the Liberal side of the House shook at Gunderson's budget, the CCF bristled when, as part of his maiden speech, J. A. Reid read a letter from one of his constituents, Albert Clotworthy.

The sixty-eight-year-old former teacher at Telkwa Elementary School maintained that British Columbia's schools were breeding grounds for pimps, thugs, dope addicts and prostitutes. Former Liberal education minister W. T. Straith shouted "slander" and the CCF baa-ed along in a rage of dreaming sheep. (They still could not understand why they weren't sitting on the government side of the House.)

Bennett's government was facing fury on two fronts: from the big companies and from liberal-minded teachers and their supporters. But the mood in the House changed. During the budget debate, Bennett called for a vote to adjourn discussion of one of Harold Winch's resolutions. For a moment, the House forgot the Socred cat-calls and the Liberal retorts, for here was a direct challenge from the premier of the province. Bennett was staking his claim to be master of the legislature. The Liberals, unwilling to risk an election, had to swallow their pride and vote along with the government. After that, insults became more personal, fights flared on a motion's notice and in the lobby of the House MLAs passed each other without a word of greeting.

Bennett's first session of the legislature had lasted for fifty-three days. His government had passed fifty-six bills despite obstructions, blunders and ill-will. His novice MLAs had blooded themselves in pursuit of his objectives and the voters outside could read the record of a government that had been as innovative as it had been sensational. Bennett was anxious to bring the session to a close before his members had reached their limits. The ninety new bills to be tabled could wait and be used to fuel a forthcoming election campaign. The session had to end leaving behind an image of a government being stifled by old tyrannies and the ever-obstructive Left. Bennett decided to send in Tilly Rolston with her Education Bill, Bill 79, to be known as the "Rolston Formula." This, with Bills 80 and 49, would amend the Public Schools Act and further the Social Credit education program which favoured the interior constituencies. The Liberals were joined by the CCF, Tom Uphill

and Bert Price, a Vancouver Socred who had his own constituency to protect. Together, they defeated the bill. The twenty-
third legislature ended three days later.

ALL THE BILLS before the legislature had passed first and
second reading except one. Named "the Rolston School
Formula" after Tilly Rolston, my minister of education, the
bill was not popular with the opposition, and they let it be
known that they would oppose it in the House. But as we had
to go ahead with our program, we had left it to the last to be
called for second reading.

When I walked into the House that night, Mr. Winch,
then leader of the opposition, asked me, "What is on the
agenda?"

I told him that the school bill was coming up for debate.
He and I had always co-operated before, and I had never taken
him by surprise. Nor had he taken me by surprise. He had his
principles and I had mine.

But now he pleaded with me to leave the bill alone,
because the estimates had not yet been completed. But I told
him we had to go ahead.

"We're going to defeat this bill, Mr. Premier," he said.

I argued that I could not see the point in bringing down
the government over this, and that we had to keep our bills
running through the legislature parallel with the estimates.

"If you want defeat, Mr. Premier," he said, "you'll get it
tonight." I smiled to myself. This could be the first step
towards a majority Social Credit government, I thought.

I went to the caucus meeting to give them a pep talk.
"This is the hour of decision," I said. "If the opposition
unites and defeats us, that'll be fine because we shall never be
able to carry out any of our policies anyway until we get a
majority. As things stand now, they can amend and destroy
any portion of any bill before a House committee. But if they
defeat us tonight, we must be ready." I concluded by saying,

"I'm ready, and I hope you are. Have you kept in touch with your ridings? Are they ready?"

Mr. Winch walked into the legislature to meet with the Conservatives and the Liberals. They thought that by bluffing, threatening to defeat us, they could stop us from bringing up the bill. As the first order of business, Tilly Rolston got up for the second reading of the "Rolston Formula" on education. In a fine twenty-minute speech she stressed the bill's good points, explaining what it meant, what it would do for the province and how it would reform the financial structure of education.

Then the storm broke. The opposition started to attack and attack again. It got increasingly bitter. But our members just sat in their seats, and let the storm blow; it blew and blew.

As each member can only speak once during a second reading of a bill, I rose to wind up the debate, after the opposition had all spoken. This was the first time I had addressed the House during the entire session. I knew that the media were waiting on my every word. I made as eloquent a plea as I could, asking the combined opposition to reconsider and pass along the bill to the House Committee, and to third reading. I said they could defeat it then, if they wished, "but pass it now; let's have further discussions in committee. The minority government seems to be getting along well, and the people of British Columbia went through an election less than a year ago; surely they don't want another one now."

There was a lot of heckling. Then, knowing that the press was there to take down everything I said, I changed my approach. Speaking very quietly, I stated, "Then you're determined to defeat the people's government tonight? The Liberals, the Conservatives and the socialists have banded together against this little people's government. All the people of the province know that Social Credit has not sought this election; it is being forced upon them by partisan politicians who dislike each other, but hate Social Credit even more. What they hate is our dynamic private enterprise system that will not give benefits to the powerful."

I said that Social Credit had been sworn in as a minority

government, holding 19 out of 48 seats, and that we did not intend to duck our responsibility, no matter how tough the going was. "We are willing to carry on and to co-operate with the opposition. People's salaries must be paid, capital works must continue! The prosperity which Social Credit wants for all British Columbians must not be impeded; let us get on with our estimates."

After the vote, we found that we had been defeated, exactly as I had expected. All during the time I was party leader and premier, I allowed all our members to vote according to their true feelings. None of them were ever told how to vote. And, as the years went by, at different times some Socreds voted against the government. But I was a little surprised when Bert Price, one of our members, stood up to vote with the opposition. It didn't make any difference, though, because the combined opposition held the majority.

The CCF, the Liberals and the Conservatives all stood up. Then I stood up to accept the vote as one of non-confidence. But I was laughing. This was a great hour of decision, and they had all been caught.

I said, "The government recognizes defeat. It recognizes that it no longer has the power to govern. It recognizes that there must be an election, but it also recognizes, as all members of the legislature recognize, that we must handle this matter with some finesse, so that nobody suffers—especially not the civil servants, the people who work for us, and the people who depend on government contracts. Therefore, I invite the leaders of all the parties to come to my office tomorrow morning at ten A.M., to discuss where we go from here. It's very important because no matter which party is elected, it will need supply money to function when it takes over power."

The three party leaders agreed to meet in my office the next morning, and the House was adjourned for two days.

When we met, I recommended we take a look at all the bills on the order paper, stating that the government would not accept any opposition bills. We could pass government bills, if the opposition agreed to accept them. All that was needed, was to let them pass without debate. As the supply estimates were not complete, I had to ask the Department of Finance to prepare an interim supply bill.

They all agreed. The supply bill was passed, section by section. The estimates were also passed. Nothing like that had ever happened before in a British parliament. They all knew that if anybody had wanted a debate, I would have moved to adjourn the House. Everything I had wanted was passed. I knew the voters would be impressed by the way I had handled things.

CCF leader Harold Winch came up to me as we were winding things up. "I'll beat you up to Government House, Wacky," he said; but I just smiled.

I knew that the opposition leaders had given the lieutenant-governor a commitment not to defeat our government without warning him in advance. I knew that, because they hadn't withdrawn that commitment; I would be able to call an election as premier. I talked to the lieutenant-governor nearly every day, and I knew he wouldn't ask Harold Winch to form a government. Mr. Winch was the opposition leader, but he had in his mind that he could line up support from the Liberals and the Conservatives, who were united against us. "Bennett's had his chance, now it's my turn," he would say. He thought the lieutenant-governor would let him dissolve the legislature, call the election and form a temporary government. That would have given him all the advantages of a ruling party during the campaign. But I knew that wouldn't happen.

I was meeting with the cabinet, when Harold Winch came to my office. Robert Worley, my executive assistant, told him I wasn't in, so he waited. As soon as I came through the door a little bell rang to let Worley know that I'd finished the meeting. Winch knew all about that bell. He walked right in, feeling no pain.

He told me that although he and the lieutenant-governor had had tea and a chat, the lieutenant-governor had turned him down. That was not surprising under the circumstances.

The Queen's representative can only have one advisor at a time, and I was that person. Constitutionally, there was no question that the Social Credit Party had the right to dissolve the legislature. But Harold didn't see it that way, and got terribly worked up about it. I had never seen him that way before.

After that, he had another battle with his own party; I think he had led them to believe that he could get the House dissolved in such a way that he'd end up being premier. Having failed in his scheme, he became sick at heart and subsequently quit provincial politics. Then he went back into federal politics. But I think the real reason why he gave up was because he had worked so hard to become premier of British Columbia, and had failed.

In many ways, I felt sorry for Harold Winch. Actually, we were good friends. Shortly after the war he and I had gone round the province together working on a rehabilitation project. That was before I was premier, during the coalition. I remember when he came over to my house for dinner one night and addressed me as "Wac" for the very first time. Then somebody else changed it to "Wacky," and that's how my nickname was born. I guess I was stuck with it, but I didn't mind.

Looking back, I would say that what Winch should have done was defeat us when the House first assembled for the session in 1952. He should have challenged Social Credit's right to appoint the Speaker, because the combined opposition did have the majority. If he had moved for somebody else to be Speaker, the motion would have carried. But I hadn't asked the opposition to second the motion to appoint the Speaker. Right there and then, I wanted to have a clear issue. That was the first resolution before the legislature, and I had to show the lieutenant-governor and the people of British Columbia that Social Credit could govern. By not opposing it, the opposition voted for it, thereby recognizing that Social Credit had the right to govern. They had in fact ducked the issue. From their position, they should have attacked the resolution right then and there. Yes, that's what they should have done.

~ 8 ~

Give Us a Chance,
Give Us a Chance

On April, 10, 1953, W. A. C. Bennett announced that British
Columbia would go to the polls on June 9. There were many
who hoped that the election results would relegate Bennett and
his "born-again" party to the opposition benches or, better
still, cast them into oblivion. The House over which he had
presided had voted $94 million for interim supply and had
passed fifty-five bills, none of them earth-shaking. Major com-
mitments such as the creation of a toll bridge authority, the
removal of milk price controls, a new liquor control act—none
of these had passed the House. Bennett's opponents were confident that he had no track record worth waving in front of the
electorate.

Yet he himself felt not a single tremor of doubt about the
forthcoming election. The issue was clear to him and the passing
of bills in the House had nothing to do with it. He was convinced
that his party was the only one in the province that could offer
the voters the kind of alternative they were looking for. His
ministers were settling in their chairs and his control in the
House was firm.

What could the opposition offer? Well, three new leaders
for a start.

The CCF wanted power and Harold Winch was simply too
old and tired to grasp it for them. They chose instead a reincar-
nation of the Reverend Robert Connell. Arnold Webster, a
mild-mannered school teacher, became CCF leader by acclama-
tion; it was a decided retreat from the fiery principles of the Old
Guard. The Red Flag was furled and stacked away in a cup-
board. Out on the hustings, the CCF wooed the voters with

82

promises of a stable economy, a contented working class and grants to create healthy and well-educated children. "If it be Christian to clothe those who are in need," said the saintly Webster, ". . . to prevent one man from dominating, bullying and exploiting another . . . if those be Christian purposes, then th CCF is a great Christian movement."

The Conservatives, on the other hand, abandoned any pretense of Christianity. Their new leader was Deane Finlayson, a former insurance agent from Nanaimo, who spoke with sounding brass but had not charity. Part of his mission was to convince the renegade Tories that he had nothing to do with the Old Guard. On the other hand, when referring to Bennett and the Socreds, his voice took on the unmistakable tones of the unlamented Anscomb. Social Credit, he was wont to proclaim, was a party of socialists—then, at another point in the same speech, he would say that the party was a refuge for fascism. He even compared Bennett to Hitler and called him "a dictator, mad for self-glorification."

The Liberals were supremely confident of their new man, Arthur Laing, who had led the Young Liberals, helped Boss Johnson into office, and was a true believer in the party. Laing told his audiences that after studying the writings of Social Credit leaders, he had found that the true issue of the election was not free enterprise versus socialism, but democratic liberalism against the McCarthyite tide of fascists and a flood of Kremlin-inspired socialists. Democratic liberalism, Laing told everyone, was the dignified option, the humane alternative to parties whose members "called each other dirty names across the floor."

Of all the parties in the election, the one Bennett feared most was his own. Though he was the political leader in the House, the election brought Albertan influence trickling back. Hansell, Solon Low and other Albertan chiefs were again looking to deliver the party into the arms of Alberta Social Credit. Although Bennett was convinced that he would win his majority this time, he was uncertain whether he could establish his mandate within the Social Credit Party.

So he campaigned as the leader around whom all banners could be raised. With Gunderson and Bonner to appease the big companies, and the small businessmen, farmers, realtors and ministers of the church on his side, he could reassure most of the people. Farmers ran in the predominantly agricultural constituencies in the Fraser Valley, the Cariboo and the Peace.

Even in the gouty confines of the old and rich Vancouver ridings, the new Socred men and women were conspicuous alternatives to worn-out models they had returned for decades.

And Bennett's presence was everywhere. It was as though he had tapped the total fund of his political knowledge. Laing, Finlayson and Webster were waifs indeed when Cecil Bennett, hesitant in speech but beaming in countenance, swept on to the speaker's platform.

CAMPAIGNING MUST BE BASED on sound logic, but it needs a spark to bring about an emotional reaction. Our theme was, "Give us a chance, give us a chance, give us the majority we need. If we don't perform well, throw us out. In fact, if we don't do a good job, I'll ask you to throw us out. Are you going to give us a chance? If you are, please stand." And they would stand.

We had a lot of people working for us. After we had won in June 1952, and people knew there was a good chance that we would form the next government, they flocked to join our party in ever-increasing numbers.

People flock to the winning side. It's like in baseball. Why do they back the winning team? Not because they're going to gain from it. No. They get a thrill from it. More and more British Columbians were beginning to see that something was really happening in their province. Without any hope for personal gain, they wanted to be part of it.

I have never used a speechwriter. If you do, you're not using your own words. Speechwriting may be acceptable for something formal, something brief. Whenever I did use a speechwriter for a statement of this type, I would always draw up the basic outline of the text beforehand, and let someone else just put some language to it.

When it came to making a speech, I could never get into the swing of it until I was heckled. Then I would challenge my adversary by bringing up a particular issue that was before the people of the province and outline the Conservatives' stand on it. I'd say, "Now any Conservative in the audience

that really believes in what they say there, please stand up."
Perhaps one or two would stand up, looking embarrassed.
Ten minutes later I'd bring up something the Liberals had
promised. "Please stand up, let people see you, be proud of it
if you believe in the Liberal platform." Half a dozen would
stand up. Then I'd turn to the socialists, the CCF. "Stand up,
my friends," I'd say, "let me see how you feel." In conclusion,
I'd bring up another issue, and again ask my opposition to
stand up. Sometimes none of them would, and I'd say to the
crowd, "You see, you're unanimous already!"

I did everything to heckle the hecklers, because I myself
had been an expert heckler. As a young man I had trained
myself how to break up meetings by heckling the speaker. I
had found out that three people could break up any meeting.
I'd place one person on the left side of the hall near the front, a
second one halfway back on the right, and a third one in the
centre of the hall. I was usually the man in the centre.

I'd get the person on the left to stand up when the speaker
was making a point. He'd get up and say, "I'm sorry, my friend,
to interrupt you, but I've come here because I want to understand your points. I'm not quite clear. Would you mind
explaining this to me, so I can understand it correctly?"

The speaker would thank him, and give the answer.

Ten or fifteen minutes later, the fellow on the right
would get up and ask another question. These were not really
trick questions, but questions where the speaker was trying to
dodge an issue.

Then, about ten minutes later, I'd get up from my seat in
the centre of the hall and I'd say, "I came to this meeting
tonight as a great supporter of the speaker. But after listening
to the answers he has given to the person up front on the left,
and to the one opposite on the right, I am beginning to
wonder whether I can support him; I think he's just an oppor-
tunist and we're being taken in. I think we should all walk out."

Of course, most of the people would get up and shout,
"Sit down, sit down," but you also get some supporters who
will say, "Give him a chance, give him a chance." You see,

human nature is very predictable. Pretty soon, half the people will walk out and that generally kills the whole meeting.

On the other hand, how do you handle hecklers when you are the speaker? The first thing you'd want to know is where your opposition is located in the audience, so that you can immediately pinpoint where the heckling is coming from. You'd start off by saying, "If there are any Conservatives here tonight, they should be proud of the Conservative Party." Then the Conservatives would applaud, and you'd know exactly where they were sitting. The same would happen with the Liberals and the CCF.

My leaving the Conservative Party and joining Social Credit had upset some young Conservative lawyers, because they felt they had helped me while I was a Conservative. I remember being invited to speak in Vancouver. Attendance was good and many people couldn't get in because the hall was so crowded. I could see my young lawyer friends sitting in a row up in the gallery. They were very, very clever, and as they knew my technique they tried to use it to their own advantage.

One of their best speakers got up and said, "Mr. Chairman, how pleased we are to have our very good friend Mr. Bennett speak to us tonight. It's so wonderful . . ." you know, and so forth, "blah, blah, blah, blah."

Then he said, "This great audience here tonight will know exactly what Mr. Bennett stands for and what his past record has been, so they'll appreciate him even more. We have seven questions we'd like to ask him. We know other people would like to ask questions too, but these questions are inter-related. Mr. Chairman, would it be possible for us to ask them all at once?"

I said, "Ask the questions all at once." Then I took my pencil, and made a note for question number one and for question number two, and then for three up to seven. Then I waited. You always want to show you're a little reluctant. He got up and said, "Mr. Bennett, answer, answer, answer."

I thanked them for asking those questions, said I was sure

the questions were clearly in their minds and in the minds of the audience. "The answer to the first question is 'yes.' The answer to the second question is 'no.' For the third question, the answer is not here, but if you write me I'll give you the information. And the fourth question is 'yes.' And the fifth question is 'yes.'" And so on, up to seven.

That started them heckling again. "That isn't what we wanted. We want our questions answered one at a time." But I kept right on going, and the crowd began to applaud. The chairman then interrupted the proceedings. "Any other questions?" he asked. That's the way you handle hecklers.

When the heckling was poor, I used to say, "What's the matter tonight? I thought we'd paid twenty dollars for each heckler; I don't think you're worth ten!"

Nobody can rise, unless it's against criticism. The media helped me tremendously in that, because criticism by the media is good. Praise kills you in public life. When people say you're good, you're wonderful, wonderful, wonderful, what's the press going to say in the next edition? They have to be critical, constructively so. Even a kite can't rise with the wind, it's got to go against it.

But the most important thing is to be sincere and show genuine enthusiasm. There is a power in people that will catch that spirit and share it with you. That was how I campaigned in 1953, and we got the majority we had asked for.

Mr. Bonner was elected in a riding that had been an opposition seat before; Mr. Gunderson ran in Oak Bay, and was ahead by a few votes on the first ballot. But, on counting the second choices, the Conservatives had backed the Liberal candidate. Therefore a Liberal was elected, and Gunderson was defeated. That was when I became minister of finance as well as premier.

The Socreds came home with twenty-eight seats. Their support had spread from the harsh interior to set the palm fronds waving in Victoria. Bennett's party had received the majority its leader had desired, and he had his own mandate of power within the Social Credit movement. True, Einar Gunderson had been defeated, but he had brushed aside the monetary theories of Major Douglas before leaving and there had been nary a protest from the minarets of orthodoxy in Alberta. Ernest Manning knew he was running a modified conservative government similar to that of Bennett, who had gained power neither through the parade-ground brutality of an Anscomb nor through readiness to grease the largest palm held out to him.

One anecdote might clearly illustrate how Bennett had managed to attract so many supporters.

Back in 1952, shortly after becoming premier, he was invited to address a chamber of commerce dinner in Nanaimo. It was, in fact, his first official function as premier. When dinner was over, Earle Westwood, the mayor of the city, pushed back his chair, stood up and began what the other guests thought was going to be a short speech to welcome their distinguished visitor. But it slowly began to penetrate their fully catered minds that Westwood was not uttering the usual platitudes. Instead, he was telling Bennett just how irate the citizens of Nanaimo were over their neglect by previous administrations, pointing to the dilapidated state of their famous old courthouse, the potholes in the roads. The mayor added that the only bridge into Nanaimo would probably fall down before materials could be brought in to repair any of the buildings.

Throughout the speech, Bennett smiled and nodded. When Westwood had finished, the other guests agreed with each other that the premier was a darn fine fellow to take such bad manners with such good grace. There was great coolness between the mayor's office and the town's prominent men for some time after that.

But Bennett did not feel he had been insulted. After all, his own limousine had bounced on some of Nanaimo's streets. Some months later, he had a call put through to Earle Westwood, inviting him to run for Social Credit in the next election. Westwood accepted, was nominated, ran and lost. But the new bridge into Nanaimo was built. In 1956 he ran again and won. A new cabinet post was created for him as British Columbia's first minister of recreation and conservation.

Bennett's steady faith was that once a man was exposed to the way *he* ran things, he would become a willing ally and producer for Bennett's cause. It was the steady faith that had pushed him from stockroom gopher to assistant sales manager

in his scant five years with Marshall Wells. It was the same faith
that had led him to build up Kelowna during the Depression
and to establish his party in Victoria and throughout British
Columbia.

But he was reaching for more than control of British
Columbia Social Credit. He knew the value of a loyal staff and
the central core of his power would be based on that. One man
would become the key to that goal. His name was William
Clancey.

BILL CLANCEY was a Liberal among Liberals, and one of our
greatest critics. I met him in 1954, during the first Grey Cup
game in Vancouver, when the Alouettes from Quebec were
playing the Eskimos from Edmonton. Clancey was enthusias-
tically promoting the event and was in charge of all the
arrangements.

I'd never seen an actual Grey Cup game before, and
during the reception and banquet the night before the game,
Clancey came over to me and said, "Mr. Premier, as you know
I've always been a Liberal, but from what I've seen of your
type of government, it is the only one that really appeals to
me. It's not for big labour, it's not for big business, and it's
against patronage. It is, however, for the ordinary people, and
I'd like to be a part of it."

One of the other Liberals present overheard Clancey's
remark; he swung round and tried to head him off. Then
someone else said, "Now, look here Clancey, what are you
saying?" Then another man whispered, "People from the
federal Liberals are here, don't talk so loud or they'll hear you."

But Clancey was unperturbed, and looking the man
straight in the face, he said, "If they're not careful and if they
don't change their ways, I'll be a Social Crediter federally as
well."

A few weeks later Clancey turned up at my office.

"I'd like to join your team," he said.

"Join the team? What do you mean, join the team?" I
asked.

"Just what I said, I'd just like to help," he replied.

"Certainly," I said, "everybody can help. We draw the circle ever larger. You can join us the same as anybody else, but don't expect any preferential treatment. In fact, if you become a good Social Crediter, it'll be harder for you to get government business than if you were a Liberal. You'll be a marked person."

Clancey joined us, but never got any business from us. At election time though, he was the best person to have around. He arranged all my campaign meetings, and every one was well attended, with hundreds and thousands trying to get in. A great organizer, that Clancey, with a great system.

Suppose we'd expect 5,000 to come to a meeting; Clancey would send out 25,000 invitations engraved with the words, "Come early if you want a seat; no seats reserved." These invitations cost money, but they fulfilled their purpose.

I'm told Clancey used to stand next to hecklers, and silence them. I never saw him do it, and I never gave him instructions to do anything like it. But he might have done it anyway. He had a lot of ways to make people turn out for meetings. He took care of all arrangements during my personal campaigns throughout the province, and I paid him for that out of my own pocket.

~ 9 ~

A Flaming Arrow

The province was large enough for everyone to swing an axe, pour concrete or drill into a rock face. There were forests to fell, roads to be laid in the wilderness, towns to spawn subdivisions and minerals to be wrested from their ancient lodes. Bennett's party had prepared no great plan for northern development; none was needed. As Phil Gaglardi said, "God put the coal there for use, so let's dig it up."

While this instinctive drive to open up the north of the province was in progress, Bennett's government drew the teeth of the socialists. He abolished health care premiums entirely, giving the people of the province completely free medical service. The monies needed for this project were found by raising the provincial sales tax. Howls rose from the press and the opposition, though neither group was excluded from free doctor's visits. The Victoria *Daily Times* professed to be shocked by Bennett's actions, stating that "the only reliable opponent of socialism has swallowed a socialist theory whole."

It was not the last time in Bennett's career that he had judged the situation correctly, letting the press trip over their own pens. The people themselves were delighted to be rid of premium payments, and the sales tax had been in effect for six years anyway.

Another flurry of tax increases that pleased the general public but goaded a few vested interests was the Assessment Equalization Act. Machinery and real property were to be taxed, and the money would be pumped into the education system. The act hit out at the large mining and logging operations whose profits had been well hidden from public view.

All these measures gave the man in the street a feeling that the new bunch in Victoria was taking care of him. Again, the press developed a touch of the socialist tingles, because while Bennett was taking a few millions out of the purses of giant companies his government was granting them logging and mineral rights on Vancouver Island and in the Peace River country.

Just behind Bennett stood the stocky figure of Pentecostal Phil Gaglardi. In his newly created post as highways minister, he became known as "Sorry Phil" for the forest of "Sorry for the inconvenience" signs that sprouted by every road and footpath in the province. Dirt roads were being paved, paved roads widened and the sign of the cloverleaf became visible wherever two major roads met. If Gaglardi had his way, not a single British Columbia hamlet would be able to call itself isolated.

What was happening to the men and women who had followed Bennett in 1952 was a process that worked deep in the political marrow of their bones. First, there had been the sheer exultation of governing. The bills they signed, the estimates they prepared, all gave them the thrill of power, but it still was an abstract thrill. Came 1953 and their great majority, and the use of power became concrete and euphoric. Now they could see rising before their eyes what their powerhouse majority in the legislature produced—schools, roads, railways, money.

To Bennett, these early years in power had an almost mystical significance. He saw the changes come about in a province the Rowell-Sirois Commission had described as a "continual and miserable drain on Confederation." He saw them as a vindication of the clean politics practised by a government of ordinary people impervious to the lures of vested interest.

But for some, the wielding of immense power and the companionship of the corporate potentates was too heady a brew. One fine Victoria morning, a Mr. Charles Eversfield, bookkeeper to a certain Mr. Gray, entered the office of lawyer David Sturdy to express concern over the favours his employer had showered on a certain minister of the Crown. He thought that these favours had led to the swift awarding of contracts, remuneration which had ended up in the pockets of Mr. Gray's friends. The minister was none other than Mr. Robert Sommers, the fire-fighting, trumpet-playing, once and future forest ranger. He had come within the orbit of Mr. Gray, a small timber and political operator—a man who introduced the right company to the right stand of trees—when he had been engaged to play trumpet at a party Gray threw in 1951 for the Big Bend

Lumber Company. The two discovered a mutual admiration for Sophie Tucker and, when Sommers was made minister of lands, forests and mines, mutual needs that Gray could satisfy with clients and Sommers with favours. Money, furniture, small chats with mighty financiers such as E. P. Taylor and even an evening watching the immortal Sophie perform were some of the lures Gray offered his friend. In return, lucrative contracts were awarded to companies Gray had recommended to the minister.

Lawyer Sturdy raised these matters with Attorney-General Bonner and later with Chief Justice Sloan. Sommers responded with slander and libel suits. The RCMP were called in and Sommers resigned. Bennett, shocked at this straying from the principles he had laid down, called in his people and delivered a fresh and stern dose of righteousness.

FIRST OF ALL," I said to our cabinet, "we are a new government. We owe no debts to any political party. We are not a political machine. We have the future completely before us.

"We shall abide by the guidelines of balanced budgets, reduce the provincial debt and cancel it altogether in seven years. With that over, we are going to be an enthusiastic government, one that will create confidence everywhere. We will get expansion going in private enterprise, the small-business field especially. We'll get labour on our side and we'll get people believing that the province is really going ahead."

I told them about the speeches I had made about real estate, how I had advised people to buy some of their own heritage, their own province if they wanted to make money. With the new development we were initiating, they were bound to make money if they used their heads and didn't buy swampland.

"You will be part of this expansion," I told them. "Grow with us! Build with us."

I spoke about building highways, bridges, towns, and the ferries. There would be freeways and great universities, not only one small one but at least three because we needed three.

My plans included building regional colleges, vocational schools everywhere throughout the province. "Our people will be trained!" I said.

I also promised to clean up the insurance mess immediately, and to work for medicare on a national and provincial basis so that nobody would ever have to fear sickness or doctor's bills. I said we would advance on all these fronts at once, and there would be no dragging of feet.

The Canadian Pacific Railway and the Black Ball Company operated a small ferry system between Vancouver Island and Vancouver, the Black Ball from Nanaimo and the CPR running a midnight boat from Victoria. Going to Vancouver from Victoria meant you'd be on the boat all night long. Another boat left Vancouver at midnight to arrive in Victoria in the morning. That was all the service they had. But even that was cancelled and moved to Nanaimo. This meant that Victoria, our capital, was left without any ferry service.

Then they had a strike up in Nanaimo against the Black Ball Company. I asked their directors if New York would advance the money to settle the strike and run a decent ferry service. I also told them what this move would do for them. But they refused because they lacked imagination and competence. So we acquired the necessary capital shares and bought them out. The CPR we left alone and they still have that one ship running from Nanaimo to Vancouver.

Then we sent Worley, my executive assistant, and others to Montreal to negotiate with the presidents of the Canadian National and the Canadian Pacific, as well as with Black Ball and Northern Navigation.

We tried to get everybody interested in a private-enterprise system, but as none of them would go along with us, we built a system ourselves. It was profitable from the first day of operation—it had to be. If you analyze it, there is Vancouver Island, the original crown colony. There is that great capital city of Victoria and here is Vancouver, our industrial heartland with a large population. And British Columbia is the best country for tourism in the world; people had to be able to move back and forth. Put in ships and you're bound to get business. So, you bring all this together, that's just common sense. Business and government are very simple; it's big companies that make it complex. They are always the poorest run.

For every problem, there is an easy solution. I will give you an example: we had no highways, no bridges, and we needed them everywhere. British Columbia is difficult terrain for road-building. You have to blast through solid rock, traverse treacherous rivers or cut through muskeg. When you drive over the Trans-Canada Highway near Burnaby you think it is as solid as the Rock of Gibraltar. But do you know what it is built on? It is built on sawdust. The foundation was so poor that we had to float it.

But a provincial premier must not just think about roads and similar local problems. I had to be interested in world trade as well, even though we were a provincial government. We knew we had great resources of coal, and there were markets which needed it in Japan, Germany and elsewhere. So we started to develop a deep-sea port on Robert's Bank, where the water was deeper than around Vancouver. How did we do it? We bought hundreds and hundreds of acres of land in that area and we started to build. All the parties—federal and provincial—were opposed to the project; so were the news media. But after awhile, the federal people saw it had some merit and they jumped on the bandwagon. We let them join us because we were never against federal involvement. We had pioneered the way so that they would come in.

We built a rail line to the port; it was owned by the government of British Columbia. We didn't want it controlled by the CN or the CPR because they would have restricted it. This way the public was carrying the cost and getting use out of it, and every other railroad could use it. We didn't try to build our railroad to the north for the reason they said we did—to get there ahead of the CNR. The CNR wouldn't move anywhere. They were pulling up lines, not putting down new ones.

We had to grow. Since 1930, our population has increased from 6 or 700,000 to 2½ million. When British Columbia joined Confederation in 1871, pushed in by Britain because it was bankrupt and they didn't want to be bothered with it anymore, British Columbia had 1 percent of the total Canadian population. In 1977 we have 11 percent of the total population and in due course we'll overtake Quebec; a few years later, we'll have even more people than Ontario.

You might say that this isn't a good thing. Look at all this unspoiled, beautiful wilderness. Of course you want to keep it that way. But I'm not thinking of the pleasures of one individual; I'm thinking of a responsibility towards the world! If people full of ambition and drive want to come to British Columbia from every province and from every part of the world, you have to let them come. Of course, you mustn't let them come faster than the economy can absorb them, but they'll become integrated if the process is properly handled.

We had an empire to build. There were various projects to the south, more to the north, while farther north was the Yukon and Alaska and beyond that our good friends, the Russians. Very important, this Canadian North. It had to be developed, had to have a railroad with the ability to carry freight. So we built it.

In 1956, Bennett again went to the polls, although the pundits felt it was a bad moment to step naked before the electorate. The Sommers case still hung in the air, unresolved, wafting tainted odours of corruption. The opposition parties were convinced they had found the spark that would ignite their fellow British Columbians and blow the Social Credit Party to kingdom come.

Out on to the vote-getting trail they sallied. Deane Finlayson, still dragging the moribund carcass of the Conservatives, had decided that the government was no longer socialistically inclined but rather a tool in the hands of monopolists. The Liberals again had Arthur Laing, who waved an olive branch at the workers, promising to rescind the tough labour legislation the Socreds had passed. The CCF ditched Webster and his Christian Socialism in favour of Robert Strachan, a tough carpenter from Nanaimo.

Once again, Bennett heard his opponents' growls with all the interest of a fisherman by a salmon-filled river, listening to the humming of gnats. He knew he was going before the electorate with an astonishing set of Gaglardi-inspired projects—a freeway from Vancouver to the United States and a four-lane tunnel under the Fraser River. The provincial coffers were brimming and "Honest" Bob Sommers had been nominated with a staggering majority by his constituents in Rossland–Trail. Let Finlayson read the charges against Sommers, let Laing fulminate and Strachan rumble on! Bennett could point to the people of Rossland–Trail and say, "They have passed judgment on Robert Sommers and have found him blameless."

Besides, Bennett by now had brought his folk-hero image to full bloom. Part of it resided in his chauffeur, whom he had inherited from Premier Johnson. George Smith was a garrulous man of indeterminate age and obscure parentage. According to him, his father and mother had drowned while fishing and he had been saved from a watery death by Indians. He had spent his childhood among them, learning their lore, carving totem poles and absorbing secrets that no anthropologist had yet discovered—or ever was likely to. In short, George Smith was a natural yarn-spinner.

Bennett, aware of Smith's love of a captive audience, used him whenever questioners became too persistent—particularly those note-pad wielders from the press. Arriving in a town where the "inquisitors" lurked, Bennett would brush them off cheerfully by saying, "Haven't time to talk right now. Ask Mr. Smith here. He has something that might interest your papers." The reporters would sigh and scribble on with determination, knowing full well that their editors would never pass on to their readers Smith's gems of folklore.

Smith also served another purpose. He had driven three premiers around the province's roads and knew the location of every pothole in them. Bennett noted the details Smith gave him. Over the years he could tell his listeners, with some truth, that their roads had been built by Phil Gaglardi and George Smith.

WE WORKED OUT A PLAN of what and where the highways should be, and then we built them over a twenty-year period. However, a lot of this construction was done in the first five or six years. Financing was difficult for the first two or three, but every year after that it became easier and easier. Not only did we pay for these roads as we went, paying off the old debt as well, but while doing so we developed surpluses of millions of dollars, which were kept in a special account. We issued loans to banks at competitive interest rates and also started all kinds of special funds, perpetual funds for causes benefiting the arts and so forth. We also set up a big sports fund which carried an annual interest. There were dozens of these funds.

Where did the money come from? From dynamic policies which produced surpluses. A stone, a large rock seems immovable. It's hard to get it rolling. But once it rolls it really moves, it gains momentum. That was the way we got our economy rolling. That's why Arthur Laing, the Liberal leader, used to call me "Bennett the Boomer."

If you have a large debt, you must plan over a seven year period to pay it back. Using surpluses, you buy back all the bonds you can get on the open market and through the stock exchanges. Then there comes a time when you can't buy any more bonds because they are in the hands of those who won't sell. So, you buy the same amount of bonds in Ontario or from the federal government or from any other province. As long as they are government guaranteed, have the same rates of interest and the same maturity dates, you can approximately offset the debt.

We had balanced budgets every year from the very first day we were in government. It didn't matter whether a Liberal, a Conservative or any other government was in power in this or that province, none of them had balanced budgets. Nobody talked or thought about it. Only we in British Columbia managed to balance our budget every year.

And all the time I was premier and minister of finance, my critics would say, "Look at that Bennett, he's an ultra-Conservative." Then, when I brought in social reforms, such as home-ownership grants, they would say, "Look, he's a Liberal." And when I had more public ownership than the

socialists had advocated, such as B.C. Hydro and the provincial
ferry service, they would say, "That Bennett, what a socialist
he is!"

I wasn't trying to be all things to all men. I was only
trying to do the job that was absolutely necessary at that time,
and I wasn't going to be tied hand and foot by a bunch of
unworkable theories.

Hitherto, Bennett had steered his relentless course with the
assurance of a born salesman, shrewd in the ways of human
nature, convinced of the excellence of his product. In 1956, he
romped home with thirty-nine members and 45.84 percent of
the voters cheering him on. One thing that must have given
him great satisfaction was that this election had been run on a
simple plurality system. No second choices had plumped Social
Credit candidates into their seats. Robert Sommers was re-elected
and seemingly any taint of wrong-doing had been removed.
But this was not the conclusion reached by Chief Justice
Sloan's enquiry. On November 21, scarcely two months after
his re-election, Sommers was arrested and arraigned. His trial
began the next year, to end three years later. Mr. Justice J. O.
Wilson called him "a scoundrel who befouled the political and
moral atmosphere for years" and sent him up to Oakalla for
five years.

For the three years the trial lasted, the Sommers case kept
surfacing to the embarrassment of the government. By the time
he was sentenced, there were voices demanding Attorney-
General Bonner's head for delays in bringing him to trial. The
press was having a field day, with the Vancouver *Sun* well out
in front predicting an early election.

During that time, the rate of growth had slowed and there
were signs of a downturn in the economy. The faint clouds of
recession brought out the Social Credit Party's fanatics, who
had been repressed by the movers and shakers during the heady
days of growth. A certain W. B. Carter, past-president of the
Silmakeen riding association, denounced the government's
legislative program as "socialistic, possibly even communistic."
A Dawson Creek extremist announced to all who would listen
that the Zionists were threatening to destroy Social Credit.

It was not the return of the flat-earth loonies that bothered

Bennett, but the defection of saner men—Cyril Shelford, for example, joined with maverick back-benchers to ask for Bonner's resignation, and then went out to back a protest by the Vancouver Dairymen's Association. Others followed Shelford's lead, and one, Mel Bryan, even walked the floor. The seeming crisis fed to the press its daily fodder. From distant Toronto, the *Globe and Mail* observed that "Bennett's famous grin" was gone.

But Bennett regarded his relations with the press as nothing more than a great game. Early on as premier he had developed an image as a fighter, always ready to take on the newspapers. As adversity hammered his government late in the fifties, he knew he could leave the press to fulminate. In British Columbia, Bennett-baiting had as little effect on the public as the comics— all they waited for was the next instalment.

As far as personal attacks are concerned, you learn to insulate yourself against them. You convince yourself that you wouldn't be doing a certain thing for personal advantage alone. As premier, you don't act for yourself, for big business or for the big labour unions. You are beyond all that, because you act for the ordinary people. If you follow that principle, you become a true populist leader, and you don't have to fear the press.

There was this fellow, I don't remember his name, who wrote a column in the Vancouver *Sun*. He always had something to say against me. That paper had been attacking me, and I demanded the right of rebuttal. They gave me a week to prepare about three pages. So I asked this chap to help me. We booked ourselves into a hotel suite in Vancouver, hired a couple of people to do the typing, set up a blackboard in the room and went into an all-night session.

At about three o'clock in the morning, this chap suddenly says that he's had enough. "What made me mad, Mr. Premier," he said, "was when you started to do all those good things for the province." And he began to enumerate them. "Instead of writing 'that's good' or 'isn't that wonderful,' I'd just get madder and madder. I'd ask myself, 'How can he do it? . . . this upstart, this Socred, when my own Liberal Party couldn't after so many years in power?' Yes, Mr. Premier, I've had enough, I'm converted."

I said to him, "I'm not writing all this stuff for you; I'm writing it for the public." After that he became a great supporter of mine.

The day after another of our victories at the polls, a reporter from the *Toronto Star* came to see me at my home in Kelowna. He said he wanted to ask me some questions.

I agreed to have a chat with him, but I knew that anything I said was never off the record.

"Where do your ideas come from?" he asked.

"You've got a radio, where does the message on the radio come from?" I replied. "The waves have always been there. You didn't discover them; they were never lost. They've been there since Creation, as far as we know. Man finds out something that has always existed, yet he thinks he's made a great discovery. Actually, he's just been stupid not to find it sooner, because it has always been there. That is one of the great laws of the Universe."

"Give me an example," he said.

I walked across the room and pulled an electric plug out of its socket. The light went out. "You see, when I plug it in the light will come on again. That law has always been there. It's not new."

The next day, the following headline appeared in the *Toronto Star*:

BENNETT PLUGGED INTO GOD

That didn't hurt me. The only people who do get hurt by such stories are those who are afraid to express their own thoughts, afraid to stick up for their own ideas.

A man is made up of many parts. More particularly, there is the part that sits above the nose; that is where he makes his great decisions, that's where his thoughts come from, especially those about the Universe, the Creation, and about human beings. That's nothing to be ashamed of; I think it is wonderful. The Great Master said to us, "There's one great force. Love!" No matter how many religions there are, no matter how many political parties there are, if they're not based on love of people, they're phony.

On July 31, 1959, W. A. C. Bennett was able to stand up and make the following announcement:

"The net Provincial Government debt of $222,453,788 at March 31, 1952, has been fully paid off or offset by equivalent sinking fund investment as of this date."

It was a statement that did not sit well in some quarters. The newspapers, for instance, claimed that Bennett had juggled the books.

Looking into figures from the Dominion Bureau of Statistics could give one the impression that British Columbia's debts were actually climbing. But, replied Bennett, those figures included such contingent liabilities as the debts of the Hydro and Power Authority and of the Pacific Great Eastern, both crown corporations guaranteed by the provincial government, yet drawing their revenues from their rates.

In 1958, the Vancouver *Province* had published a story accusing him of finagling his figures. Bennett had responded with a lawsuit. The sum of $1 million in damages was bandied about, and the newspaper owners retracted the story. They even printed the retraction as a headline.

The next year, W. A. C. Bennett had no fear of reporters bemused by figures or by what anyone else could say. He planned to demonstrate in terms anybody could understand just what British Columbia had done through his government.

DURING MY TWENTY YEARS in office as premier of the province, we celebrated many occasions and many great anniversaries. But our finest hour came when we were able to rejoice about having paid off the entire debt our province had incurred throughout all administrations prior to Social Credit's. We had done it in seven years. I don't claim to be a Bible scholar, but this much I know: seven is an important number and cycles of seven appear throughout the Scriptures.

On August 1, 1959 it was exactly seven years to the day since the lieutenant-governor of British Columbia had sworn us in as the new provincial government. On that day I invited everyone to my home town, Kelowna, for a giant bond-burning ceremony. We were going to "burn up the debt." They came in large numbers, the turnout was terrific and amazed everybody.

We sent the bonds in trucks from Victoria to Kelowna and then out to a barge moored on Okanagan Lake. It was a beautiful summer evening and the shore was lined with thousands of people, thousands and thousands who had flocked from all over British Columbia when they had heard the good news. People came from everywhere, some to celebrate, some just to watch or to be able to say, "I was there."

Einar Gunderson came. He wanted to know how I was going to start the fire.

"The RCMP's going out there to the middle of the lake and they'll light a match," I said. "That will make the bonds burn."

"I think you should be a little more dramatic," he said. "If I were you, I would use a bow and arrow—a flaming arrow—to light the fire."

"I don't know," I said. "I haven't pulled a bow or shot an arrow for many, many years."

"Well, you'll be up close and if you miss, it would be interesting in any case," he insisted.

"That's fine," I said. "Get me a flaming arrow and a bow and we will do it."

But because the bonds were so tightly packed in the barge, we thought they wouldn't burn. So we added a lot of straw and soaked them in oil. Then the barge was towed out to the middle of the lake so that we wouldn't start any land fires.

We got into a boat at the wharf and went out to the barge. When we got close to it, I pulled the bow and this flaming arrow shot through the air. It hit the barge. Our critics said we missed but there was no way we could have as we were so close. However, to contain the straw and not have it scatter all over the countryside, we had bound it tightly with wire netting, small-mesh chicken wire, lots of it. The arrow hit the wire and bounced right back into the lake.

I suppose that was why they said we'd missed; but of course that wasn't true. We had hit the wire. Anyway, we had the RCMP there in their little boat and they carried matches. They lit the fire, and when the flames shot up the people all cheered. It was a glorious occasion.

After that, everyone knew forevermore that the first Social Credit government of British Columbia had paid off all their debts. None of them were transferred to contingent liabilities, no matter what the critics said. Certainly, we guaranteed our crown corporations. We had our liabilities just like Ontario had with their Hydro or Quebec had with theirs. Every province provided guarantees which brought about contingent liabilities. But the guarantees won't pay them off; you have to pay them. The only reason why you have to guarantee is because you want your corporations to get their loans at low rates of interest.

Our critics tried to tell us we had only transferred the debt, that we had not really paid it off. They said, "Bennett has three sets of books—and just wait until he loses power and we can look in and see them." Very peculiar; after the socialists became the government in 1972, they looked into the files but couldn't find those three sets of books. Sure enough, the debt had been paid off in 1959, just as we had said it was.

~ 10 ~
Lots and Lots of Water

At one of the many cocktail parties William McAdam of British Columbia House in London was called upon to attend, he happened upon Bernard Gore, the financier, who represented Axel Wenner-Gren, a Swedish industrialist. The two men chatted amiably and McAdam was moved to extol the virtues of British Columbia's rivers, its mighty forests and mineral-rich rocks. The financier might have yawned through the descriptions of snow-capped peaks, but the mention of streaks of zinc, copper, lead and gold just waiting to be dug up made him listen. Shortly after, Bernard Gore and Birger Strid, another Wenner-Gren man, turned up in Victoria to speak with W. A. C. Bennett, the premier of the land whose rocks held such riches.

It was 1954 and Bennett was mired in the Sommers scandal, internecine party rifts and arguments with substantial areas of the province. The words of Strid and Gore conjured a path out of his miseries. They had a development package in mind— great dams could appear where none had been before, massive logs could roll down slopes and onward to smoke-belching sawmills; towns could spring up where the deer now browsed and an aerial monorail could carry the inhabitants of this great new northern wonderland to their destinations at speeds approaching 180 miles an hour.

Faster than a speeding rail car, Bennett grasped that these men had visions that flew as high as his own. Moreover, he could use their schemes to complete a vast manoeuver he was beginning to execute.

It took three years to forge a deal with Axel Wenner-Gren,

105

a man after Bennett's own heart. When lands, mines and forests minister Ray Williston stood up in the House to announce that a "Memorandum of Intent" had been signed with the Swedish magnate, it also came to light that Wenner-Gren had made his first millions from the Krupp munition cartel during the war and had dined with Hermann Goering at the Nazi minister's sumptuous country hideaway.

Bennett was up to his ears in bad press again, but he stood by the $5 million deal to cover a preliminary survey of 40,000 square miles of land. In return, the government handed Wenner-Gren land and mineral reserves along the proposed monorail route, an area five to twenty miles wide and four hundred miles long, and added water reserves on the Peace, Parsnip and Findlay rivers. Handing over these water reserves was part of the plan the premier held behind his back as he stood to face his critics each day in a wildly inflamed legislature. Development of the Peace was one part of the picture, clearing the provincial debt was another, but only Bennett knew what the whole picture was to be.

WE HAD TO FIND JOBS for people and that meant we had to have industry, for which you need hydro-electric power. At that time, there was no surplus power. We needed to develop power lines and generating stations everywhere if we wanted to attract industry to British Columbia.

I began to look at two rivers, the Columbia and the Peace. Negotiations between the United States government and ours had been going on about the Columbia for forty or fifty years, but they were getting nowhere. The Columbia is in the southern part of the province—in the drought area. It's all right to have a watershed there, but to complete it you need another watershed in an area where there is an abundance of rain. Then, no matter what happens elsewhere, you will always have lots and lots of water. The place that had lots and lots of rain, lots of water and lots of snow was Northern British Columbia.

The Peace River flows through Northern British Columbia, north to the Arctic Ocean. I began to study the whole subject. One day, I went up to have a look at the Peace, which then was a little muddy river. I went to a little town called Fort St. John, which was a very small place in those days. Some RCMP men drove me along a dusty trail to the shores of the river. I stood on the high banks looking down and I saw something. . . . The Mounted Police had left me alone and I just stood there looking down. Along came a trapper, with a pack on his back, and he stopped. He had been staring at me for quite a while. Then he came over to talk to me. "Mister, what are you looking at?"

"Have you been looking that way too? What do you see?" I asked.

"I see a muddy little river that has been running on for centuries and centuries. I come through here all the time because I have a small trap line. . . . But what do *you* see?"

"Well," I said, "I see cities, prosperous cities, beautiful schools and hospitals, universities. I see women doing their baking in ovens that use electricity. I see thousands of jobs all resulting from what you and I are looking at right now."

He asked me one or two more questions and then he said, "You know, up in this north country, we get a lot of crazy people coming here. But you are the most craziest person that ever came into the north as far as I am concerned."

I said, "Thank you very much." And away he went.

Isn't it funny. One person can see something, an opportunity, a chance; and another can only see the mud.

We knew that from the Peace River we could create the largest man-made lake in Canada, a great reservoir for fresh water. The greatest thing we need in our civilization, in our time, is not oil, not gas, but fresh water; not just any old water but *fresh water*. There's too little of it in the world. We're heading into a period of droughts. I am not prophesying doom, but we should be prepared, we should be storing as much water as we can.

These people who are always criticizing dams don't know what they are talking about. We should be encouraging the building of dams everywhere in Canada. Of course, we shouldn't hurt our natural resources such as our fish. Of course, we should protect our natural beauty at the same time, but we should encourage dams to be constructed even for farmers on their ranches. If water flows through an area, build a dam! Governments should encourage that, because what is needed is an abundance of fresh water.

The Peace River Country was the solution to our problems. And in the south we had another great opportunity on the Columbia River. Both sites had to be developed at the same time because we were heading for an inflationary period, which would escalate costs during construction time. As I went around the world, I learned that the forces of inflation were being unleashed once again; let loose uncontrollably, they could destroy our whole civilization.

We had to race against time, to get some of this power developed before costs increased more and more. We encouraged the federal government, first the Conservatives and then the Liberals who succeeded them, to carry on negotiations with the United States so that we could get the Columbia development going at the same time as the Peace River. If we hadn't done so, if we had waited with the project until today, it would have cost at least $2½ billion more.

The vision of Wenner-Gren Land faded and merged with the Peace River idea. Looking down at the Peace River in 1957, Bennett announced that "the greatest hydro-electric project in the world" would be built there. A massive dam would be reared and British Columbia would receive power more cheaply than any other place in the world.

Observers noted that his remarks were thrown both at the electorate and, over his shoulder, at the federal government in Ottawa. Between bursts of Peace River visions, Bennett denounced the stalled negotiations between Ottawa and Washington over the Columbia River project, calling the numerous meetings between their negotiators "pink teas on the Rideau."

The news that Bennett was up to something on the Peace River puzzled rather than shocked the Ottawa mandarins. They could hardly see what use could be made of the Peace, as it ran in the wrong direction, northward across the eastern Rockies to join the great Mackenzie in its trek to the Arctic Ocean. Nor could they see how Bennett would transmit the power, providing he could generate it, from the Peace to southern British Columbia. No, they concluded, Bennett would have done better to have stayed with them on the Columbia River project. Although it had been hard sledding, soon the prime minister of Canada and the president of the United States would sit down to sign the treaty for the dams to go up. Far-sighted federalism would bring the benefits home to British Columbia despite its obstreperous premier.

But the negotiations dragged on for seven more years.

The Columbia River had always posed a problem to the makers of hydro-electricity, a problem created by nature and compounded by man. The glaciers were at the bottom of it. As they had retreated northward, their clubbed feet had drawn deeper and deeper gouges in the surface of the earth. Farther south, where their weight had rested for only a few thousand years, their passage had left rolling hills and gentle valleys. To the north, their weight had sat thousands of years longer, marking the earth with cataracts and deep gorges. Here, the Columbia became a white-water river, known to the Indians and early settlers as a place of wearying portages. Later, the plans of nations complicated its course—between the savage upper reaches and the placid ox-bows to the south, Washington and Ottawa drew a line making the upper Columbia Canadian and the lower, American.

Time passed and industry came to the lower Columbia. The Americans had built beyond their power needs and looked to take energy from their sometimes respected neighbour to the north. But Sir Wilfrid Laurier had anticipated all this when he concluded the Boundary Waters Treaty with the United States. The 1909 treaty called for a great deal of discussion before a pint of anything was given away cheaply to someone else.

The Americans built a series of dams on the lower Columbia, the largest and most famous among them being the Grand Coulee. But more would be needed. In 1940, Mackenzie King had agreed to the creation of an International Joint Commission that would explore the uses of water between Canada and the United States. The Columbia was a major topic on the agenda. The Americans explained that the glaciers had created a dilemma for them. None of the dams and generating stations they had built on the lower reaches of the river could produce to capacity because of the wide variance in the river's flow. In winter, the water came in a trickle; in spring and summer, the runoffs caused floods. They proposed a series of dams on the Canadian side that would act as catchments to store the water. This would realize the power potential of the lower Columbia, and in return, the Americans would make some of that power available to energy-poor British Columbia.

Four years later, General "Andy" MacNaughton became chairman of the Canadian commission. He did not like the American proposals for the Columbia, but favoured a diversion of both the Columbia and the Kootenay into the Fraser so that their northward flow would create electricity within Canada and massive supplies of fresh water for the drought-prone Prairies. The Americans protested. Such a diversion would interfere with their use of the water downstream. But they were hamstrung by the clause their own negotiators had forced on Sir Wilfrid Laurier back in 1909. According to that clause each country could do what it pleased with its own waters.

MacNaughton's plan was still under discussion in 1960. The revised proposal called for the diversion of the Kootenay into the Columbia; the water would turn turbines installed at the Mica dam site, which would serve as the main point of power generation in the system.

The Americans countered with proposals for a dam at Libby, south of the border, where power could be generated by waters diverted to their side of the watershed. But the Canadians were no more willing to permit the Americans to usurp Canada's upstream privileges than the Americans were willing to let the lion's share of the water stay in Canada.

In late 1960, W. A. C. Bennett arrived at the U.S.-Canadian conference table fresh from a narrow election victory. Two of his cabinet ministers had been kicked out and the number of Social Credit seats had been reduced to thirty-six. He needed a success to keep his banners flying. The Mica dam, he realized, would generate power at a cheaper rate than his own Peace River scheme. If Mica went ahead, the Peace was doomed. He plumped for the American proposal. MacNaughton, horrified and outraged, retired to Ottawa denouncing Bennett for having allowed the Americans to walk "into a house divided against itself and skin the occupants alive."

Everyone was furious with W. A. C. Bennett—everyone except John G. Diefenbaker, the Prince Albert visionary who was currently sitting in the prime minister's seat watching the lights go out in every part of his vision and realizing that they were unlikely to be lit again at the next election. Concluding that a speedy end to the Columbia negotiations might save him, he charged off to Washington to persuade U.S. president Dwight D. Eisenhower to put his signature on the draft proposal of the treaty. Over the muffled wails of the CCF, now the New Democratic Party, the federal parliament ratified the treaty, which was then sent to Bennett in British Columbia for signature.

But Premier Bennett did not sign. There was anguish in Ottawa and bafflement in Washington. The Americans failed to see how one elected politician in what appeared to be an appendage of Canada could hold up the majesty of the presidential seal by professing to have second thoughts. In actuality, Bennett was having third and fourth thoughts about the Columbia River development. He dug in to protect his idea of a two-river system in which the Peace development would be the primary producer of electricity and the Columbia a trump card to be held in reserve. The wily premier was ahead of both Ottawa and the Oval Office; in fact he was twenty, even thirty years ahead of them. He was bucking for a treaty that would last longer than that.

WE PLANNED TO BUILD three dams in British Columbia to control the waters that flowed from the Columbia across the American border and eventually to the Pacific Ocean. We would control it, and by controlling it, we would make the American power developments more valuable as time went by. We ourselves would be able to get increased power development because we would control the three dams. For the first time in B.C. history, we would get all the power developed in our own province and half of that developed in the United States. No other province had concluded a similar deal.

The Peace River was being developed and we had an abundance of hydro-electric power. But the criticism we had to listen to was terrible! First, about the Peace. They said you could never transmit power over that distance to Vancouver, the place where most of it would be needed and used. No, the distance was far too great!

They had no vision. We stood alone against all the other parties, the federals, other provincial governments, even the United States. They opted only for the Columbia; but we alone said that the Peace was vital for our province. Today, 90 percent of the power used in British Columbia by B.C. Hydro comes from our Peace River development, the one they had said we could never utilize. It's tremendous!

Since we had more power from the Columbia than we could sell or use in B.C., we sold to the United States our half share of it, but only for the duration of the first half of the treaty—for the next thirty years.

We sold that power for cash and invested the money. We loaned $100 million to the province of Quebec for awhile. Invested wisely elsewhere, our assets grew from the original amount to $500 million. It paid for the dams and for a lot of other development, such as in the Kootenays. As a result, British Columbia became a better country than it had ever been before.

Now, the critics say it didn't pay for all the cost of the dams, this cash we received from the Americans. It was a sell-out to the Yankees, they say. The answer to that accusation is that of all the treaties ever concluded between Canada and a foreign country, this one was the best for British Columbia *and* for Canada. The critics could only see the first half of the treaty but the agreement covers sixty years, not thirty. We were only paid for the first half.

What about the last half of the treaty? Well, even the Canadian Broadcasting Corporation was badly fooled, when they produced those documentaries about the "disaster" of the Columbia and what it meant for British Columbia and Canada. How stupid these people are. They always forget about the last half of the treaty when the United States must give back to us at our border our share of the power, our rightful half. Whatever they've developed over thirty years, half of it comes back to us either in power or in cash. The Americans have no choice in the matter, it's our choice, our decision. That's going to amount to a lot of money, one day, especially since inflation hurt us while we were building the dams. But

it will help us during the last half of the treaty. The power
will be worth ten times more than what we thought it would
be worth way back then. It's going to be worth tens and tens of
millions of dollars. The Americans will have to give it to us,
either in cash or in power. Yes, it is a tremendous treaty, the
best for the people of this province and for our country.

Bennett knew that Diefenbaker was becoming isolated from, if he
was not already at odds with, the civil service in Ottawa. He also
knew that the Tories were separating into factions and that the
only one he had to fear was the one led by Davie Fulton, a native
British Columbian.

Fulton was justice minister in the Diefenbaker cabinet.
Together with Howard Green, another British Columbian, he
had negotiated the draft Columbia River treaty. But Bennett
wanted to rip it up to plough ahead with his own proposals.
His idea was to sell the Columbia power back to the Americans;
British Columbia would use the power on the Peace.

He fired his opening guns when he flew into Seattle to
attend a political testimonial banquet also attended by President John F. Kennedy and his entourage. Bennett beamed
when Senator Mike Mansfield, the U.S. Senate majority leader,
introduced him as the prime minister of British Columbia.
Bennett closeted himself with Kennedy and five days later was
gratified to hear the U.S. secretary of the interior, Stewart
Udall, denounce Fulton's opposition to Bennett's grand plan
as "stuff and nonsense."

Fulton flew to Victoria to see the recalcitrant premier, but
Bennett, though seen minutes before the minister's plane
landed, was not around to greet him. Fulton kicked his heels
around the parliament buildings for awhile and then returned
to Ottawa.

Bennett's carefully aimed lob landed right in the Diefenbaker dugout. This time, the Chief sent Donald Fleming out to
see the errant premier. Bennett greeted him with smiles and his
very own presence and ushered him out two days later, still
smiling. Fleming, however, had little to smile about. The
message he had to drag back was that Ottawa could either build
the dams alone and do what it liked with the power, or British
Columbia would build them alone and sell the power back to
the Americans. Fleming called it an ultimatum; for once,

Diefenbaker's ministers saw things clearly. It was an ultimatum and Bennett was perfectly capable of carrying it out. Not for nothing had he burnt the raft of paid-up bills on Okanagan Lake! British Columbia could borrow the money to pay for the dams anywhere in the world; Ottawa, after various financial fiascoes, could not.

There was only one hitch in Bennett's plans. He could produce the power on the Peace, but he couldn't find a buyer for it. The British Columbia Electric Company controlled the most lucrative markets, and its board was a creature of Ottawa. Bennett had old scores to settle with the company because of its slow development of the province's hinterland. It was a Vancouver-based, federally dominated roadblock that stood right in the path of Bennett's wagon—and he knew how to deal with it.

B RITISH COLUMBIA ELECTRIC COMPANY distributed 90 percent of the province's hydro-electric power. It didn't have the vision for the kind of growth our province needed. That is why we were developing power from the Peace River with private funds.

We had this chap come from Sweden—Wenner-Gren. He had an idea and his company sent engineers up there, who joined forces with a team of British financial geniuses. They had the assets to form a company they called the British Peace River Power Development Corporation. British Columbia Electric Corporation was one of their shareholders at the time and I understood there was fair co-operation between them.

Six months went by and the new corporation did nothing. That didn't fit in with my schedule, as I was afraid of inflation. At the time, Sir Andrew McTaggart, an Englishman from London, was the head of the company. He came to B.C. from time to time, but as I was worried I decided to take a trip to London myself.

When I arrived there, I asked Sir Andrew, "Why does everything stay still? I can't understand why development is held up."

W.A.C. Bennett at the opening of the 1955 Kelowna Regatta.

Bennett politicking in 1958.

A 1961 studio photo of the B.C. premier.

Left, The original Bank of British Columbia was housed in this building in Victoria; constructed circa 1887.

Below, Aerial view of the Hugh Keenlyside Dam near Castlegar, on the Columbia River System.

Opposite, Two views of the 600-foot-high Bennett Dam, part of B.C. Hydro's Peace River project which has created British Columbia's largest lake, covering more than 400,000 acres.

Budget Day, 1962. W.A.C. Bennett speaking in the B.C. Legislature.

Opposite, A surprised W.A.C. is trapped into shaking hands with Tory leader Derril Warren, just after announcing the date of what would be his last election.

Cecil and May at their
Kelowna estate and on
their 50th wedding
anniversary in 1977.

He told me that no matter how strong a company was financially, it couldn't proceed with a project such as the Peace River without prior contracts for power. "And we can't get contracts," he said.

"Who do you need contracts from?" I asked.

"You know there's only one corporation that really has the right to sell power in British Columbia, and that's British Columbia Electric."

"They're your shareholders," I told him. "You mean to tell me that they won't give you a contract, not even on a negotiated basis, on a basis to be settled by the courts?"

"No," he replied. "They won't agree to contract any power with us at any price or on any terms. They're controlled and told what to do by the two federal parties in Ottawa, the Conservatives and the Liberals. They just want the Columbia development and don't want anything to do with the Peace. They'd rather the Peace not go ahead."

I knew that Dr. Grauer, the head of the British Columbia Electric happened to be in Europe at the time. He was also head of our university, a good citizen. I said to Sir Andrew, "Dr. Grauer is over here somewhere."

"Yes," he replied. "Yes, I was talking to him this morning."

"Where is he?"

"He's in Paris."

"Well, arrange for him to fly over. This is urgent. Arrange for him to fly over to London immediately. Tell him to have breakfast with me in my suite at eight tomorrow morning."

"Yes," said Sir Andrew, and he did that.

They came to my suite, had breakfast, and then I had McTaggart explain exactly what he had told me, but this time in front of the head of British Columbia Electric. Then I said to Dr. Grauer, "I am not talking to you as your friend now, nor as your enemy either. I am talking to you as the premier of the province of British Columbia. So be careful how you answer, because a lot depends on it. Is what McTaggart told me correct?"

"Yes."

"Can't you contract on a basis of negotiation for power and development? Isn't that the way it should be? It's in the terms of the contract."

"No—no way."

Then I said to both of them, "There's a great law of nature that goes something like this—what you don't use, you lose. If a person is a pianist and doesn't develop it, he loses his talent. If a person is a good pitcher in baseball and doesn't throw, he loses that talent. We are not going to sit by and watch potential development in British Columbia be held back by any source, not by big business, not by big labour, not by big government. I want you to clearly understand that. I will give you reasonable time but it will be short."

They didn't do anything. In due course, I called a special session of the legislature in Victoria. We had prepared the necessary bills in a confidential way because we didn't want to do anything that would affect the markets. We brought the bill in, effective as of that day, but from midnight the night before. It was for a takeover of Peace River Power Development, taking over on behalf of the province—and we included B.C. Electric. Now that was unusual for us, because we were the number one private enterprise government anywhere. We had to do it though, not take over one concern but the whole thing, so that thousands and thousands of smaller concerns would have a chance to develop and grow in British Columbia.

We offered a price for B.C. Electric because it was a federal power corporation that owned it—the Federal B.C. Corporation. B.C. Electric was its subsidiary. We had to offer a price because we couldn't take it over directly. The price per share we offered was higher than the market; not too much higher, but enough. It was a fair deal for the shareholders. We put that right in the bill.

They took us to court. It was their duty to do that, the

proper thing. I didn't mind at all. There were lots of arguments, and in due course the chief justice brought down his
decision. The amount was only what we had offered—plus a
reasonable profit for the period of litigation, or reasonable
interest for the period; same thing really.

The press came after me. What was the government going
to do? I said, "Of course we believe in the courts, of course we
will abide by the judge's decision. Not only will we abide by the
chief justice's decision but we will accept the chief justice's
interpretation of the zones of interest. In that way, there will
be no question of misunderstandings." And that's what
happened.

~ 11 ~

A New Bank

Bennett had the pleasure of seeing *Barron's*, America's leading business and financial weekly devote its entire front page to him and his two-river project. Its comments were less than flattering to him, for his actions were compared to those of Fidel Castro and his province to "a so-called People's Republic." He even made the London papers, and the *Sunday Telegraph* thought Canada was acquiring the financial reputation of a banana republic.

The lengthy court case cooled down the atmosphere as public interest palled before legal windiness. Attorney-General Bonner geared his staff to fight a delayed and devious action— one which at one point saw the socialists actually defend the rights of British Columbia Electric shareholders. On Monday, July 29, 1963, a day the *Province* declared in banner headlines as "Black Monday for Bennett," matters were finally settled.

For Bennett, it wasn't "Black Monday" at all for he had been prepared to reward the shareholders handsomely if Chief Justice Lett so decreed. The judge and the premier saw eye to eye, and the settlement came to just less than $200 million, only $30 million more than Bennett had offered two years earlier. He was quite satisfied. His government's reputation of being beholden to no one shone as brightly as before.

As for his Peace River business, events moved in such a way as to fill Bennett with glee. MacNaughton was removed from the International Joint Commission, and in the federal election of June 1962 the Diefenbakerites limped back into minority, strongly supported by the federal Social Credit Party. Davie Fulton was brought down from his lofty post as justice minister to become the man who looked after public works. Diefenbaker followed this up with a Throne Speech announcement that long-term contracts for the export of power would be allowed, indeed encouraged.

It was not enough, for Bennett knew that the Conservatives were about to topple and that Lester B. Pearson would soon become prime minister. Pearson had made more than polite noises to John F. Kennedy during the Nobel Prize dinner that the president had hosted in Washington, promising a protocol to the treaty, that is, additional drafts acceptable to Bennett and Kennedy having the same legality as the original Columbia treaty. Pearson led the Liberals back to victory in April 1963. The Columbia and the Peace River treaties were finally signed, sealed and delivered to Bennett. He had got what he wanted.

In the fall of 1963, he had his own election to contest, and this time he was threatened with a four-party fight. The Conservatives had rid themselves of Deane Finlayson and were awaiting the return from Ottawa of their native son Davie Fulton, who had left the good ship *Diefenbaker* shortly before it sank. When Fulton announced he would stand for provincial leadership and give "that arrogant man" the drubbing of his life, local Tories danced for joy. So did the provincial New Democrats, who foresaw a splitting of the free-enterprise vote. Their leader, Robert Strachan, was toned down, buttoned up and sent out to woo the moderates. But the vote did not split; it solidified. Fulton lost to Gaglardi and the Conservatives remained without a member in the legislature. W. A. C. Bennett breezed home, his policies vindicated and his party stronger than before.

In September 1964, W. A. C. Bennett stood under the Peace Arch at Blaine, Washington to receive a cheque for $253,929,534.25 from the hands of U.S. president Lyndon Baines Johnson in payment for British Columbia's share of the Columbia's downstream power. The Texan told the crowd that the Canadians had taken him for his last quarter, and Bennett, at his side, glowed rather than merely beamed. But he wanted something more for British Columbia.

A$_{LL MY LIFE}$, since I was a small boy, I was interested in banking. I knew that it was of prime importance to any business, any economy, any government and any country.

The lack of a good banking system had held us back in the Depression days. Not that we could have avoided a world depression, but we could have weathered the storm much better if we had built a banking system that would have protected our people.

Canada had given charters to banks, ten-year charters which gave them the sole right to print money and control credit over and above the one-dollar bills. After the First World War, which had badly muddled up finances, the Economic Division of the League of Nations had recommended that countries without central banks set them up; such a system would steady their economies when necessary. That was back in 1921. Canada couldn't set up a central banking system then because the charters didn't expire until 1923. By that time, the Liberal party was in power and Mackenzie King had become prime minister. I admit he did many good things for Canada, but by giving the banks their same old charters for another ten years instead of setting up a central bank, he committed a grave error.

When we slid into the Depression in 1929, we ended up with a wheelbarrow instead of a truck to deal with our financial problems. We had no way of financing ourselves through it all, because the charters remained in force until 1933.

My namesake, R. B. Bennett, became prime minister in 1930. He set up a royal commission to look into the possibility of founding a central bank. By the time it got going, it was January 1935. I was nominated to the board of directors but did not get elected despite my great interest and my earlier efforts to promote central banking.

This Bank of Canada was a great thing, but it didn't do R. B. Bennett any good at the time because the Depression was so severe. He kept coming up with all sorts of promises, and even went socialist in his reforms. But people no longer believed him; they'd had four years of him and his Bennett Buggies out on the Prairies. They defeated him in 1935.

The central bank remained. We had a central bank in Ottawa and various banks in eastern and central Canada. Not a single bank had its headquarters in Vancouver. That caused problems. If anyone was trying to get a loan in British Columbia, they'd have to phone to the East. It could be a lovely sunny day in Vancouver, but if it was snowing and freezing in Toronto and Montreal your loan would be turned down.

I tried hard to get some of the banks to move their headquarters to Vancouver, but they all refused. So we decided to establish a new bank.

Great Britain had originally founded a Bank of British Columbia back in the early days. In fact, it was the first bank to open its doors in San Francisco. It did business there because British Columbia was so close. It went bankrupt later for lack of capital, or lack of judgment, I guess. The Bank of Commerce bought its assets but not its name.

We wanted to set up a new Bank of British Columbia with headquarters in Vancouver, a bank fully chartered by the federal government. I went to Ottawa to see Prime Minister Pearson. I knew him well. He had been a good foreign minister and we had done a lot of negotiating on the Columbia River project. He agreed with me that British Columbia needed its own bank and I explained to him that it would be under federal jurisdiction. Then he asked me how many shares my government would want to buy.

"Twenty-five percent," I said. "We'll offer it to the public and we won't allow anybody to gain control. No Canadian will be stopped from buying in, but we want to retain 25 percent."

He asked me many more questions and I answered them all.

His government agreed and we went ahead with all the preparations. Then one day, the prime minister advised me our 25 percent control couldn't be allowed because there had been a lot of pressure from the other banks. The most we could buy, he said, was 10 percent.

I agreed. He tried to get that passed, but in the end they would not allow us any of the voting shares.

Our charter had to be approved by the Senate, and we were having a hard time getting it through. Then, one day, Senator David Croll came to see me.

"Bennett," he said, "you're not going to get your bank charter."

"What do you mean?" I asked. "I thought the government was all for it."

"Is that so?" he replied. "If the East Block would give us the green light, we'd pass it in thirty minutes."

I knew Paul Martin, one of the ministers in the Liberal government, even better than I knew Mr. Pearson, and I went to see him.

"One thing I know about you, Paul Martin," I said, "although we may have different political views and lots of arguments, you do not lie. Senator Croll, one of your colleagues in the Senate, told me that the prime minister's office is not giving us the O.K."

He paused for a little while and then said, "Croll shouldn't have told you that."

"You know it's true, don't you?" I replied.

He nodded.

Then I got mad. "You Liberals claim to be a people's government? You're hand in glove with big finance! I know that many of the people in the Senate are represented with the other chartered banks. I'm going to turn this country upside-down and no way will I keep quiet about this!"

What talks Martin had with the prime minister and the cabinet, I don't know. Anyway, it wasn't long before our charter was approved by the Senate.

I knew that a bank in Vancouver would help the development of the province and western Canada as a whole. And the other chartered banks, by force of competition, would have to allow their people in Vancouver to grant loans to help the economy. We set up the Bank of British Columbia, which has a large number of branches in our province as well as in Alberta.

Financing and banking are important to the expanding economy of any country. They were vital to British Columbia.

The Russians
are Coming

Things in the province were booming in a style that dwarfed its previous rate of growth. The ultimate accolade came when *Time* magazine decided to make British Columbia's bonanza its feature story in both the American and the world editions. Premier Bennett's picture was on the cover and he appeared on most of the inside pages of the magazine. Later that month, he was invited to dine with *Time* publisher Henry Luce before hopping off to Germany to receive a medal from the Bavarian government in recognition of his achievements.

Looking back, Bennett could see how the blacktopping of dirt roads had led to the construction of a power dam bigger than Egypt's Aswan project. The government of "zanies and funny-money wavers" had become the owners of a railway, a fleet of ferries, a provincial bank and a system of highways that rivalled the complexities of the freeways of Los Angeles. A squadron of aircraft was at hand to carry Bennett's ministers about the provinces and, if necessary, around the world. They moved in a style almost befitting plenipotentiaries of a sovereign power.

Bennett had set a pace that other provincial governments were only beginning to follow. Before him, provincial ministers scarcely travelled at all unless it was to take a rail trip to Ottawa. He had initiated the custom of letting the provincial head bargain in person over who would develop what within the province. In Tokyo, he sipped tea with the heads of the Japanese Greater Co-Prosperity Combines; in Germany, he slapped the backs of industrialists and indulged in his non-alcoholic beverages while the Rhine wine flowed.

But unlike many present-day politicians who are off to the tropics at the drop of a snowflake, Bennett was a man for all seasons. He would trudge through the snow anywhere to sell British Columbia to a potential investor. And having sat down with American, West German and Japanese capitalists, he was equally happy to entertain those who came from the other side of the Iron Curtain.

IN THE EARLY DAYS, the Russians in Canada weren't allowed to travel beyond the immediate vicinity of Ottawa. Their representatives, military men, economists and so on, were stationed there. They were perhaps the best and keenest minds they had at the time. The Russians wanted them as watch-dogs in Ottawa, as close to the U.S.-Canadian border as possible, because they couldn't be in the United States.

Somehow, the Russians had heard about Social Credit in British Columbia. Word had reached me that they would like to see me, in fact, come to Victoria to meet me. Would that be possible? I said yes and arrangements were made.

As I had heard that they weren't allowed to travel more than fifty miles from Ottawa, I wondered how they would get to British Columbia; they would need a permit, I thought, and I spoke to Bonner, my attorney-general, about it. He just laughed and said that the Russians were not allowed to leave the Ottawa region.

"Contact the police and tell them the Russians are coming," I said.

When Bonner went to the RCMP and told them about it they just laughed. But the Russians were going ahead with their plans anyway and soon a message reached me confirm-ing the date of their arrival.

I again spoke to Bonner. "I want you to be at my office at ten o'clock on Saturday; in fact, be there at a quarter to ten and bring along your camera. The Russians will be there taking pictures and I want you to take two pictures for every one of theirs. This is going to be an interesting day, Bob."

"They're not coming," he scoffed.

But I went on. "I want plainclothes men everywhere, no military uniforms, no Mounties in uniform; and I want you to have somebody drive your car because we're going off in mine to see the sights."

I wanted to treat them well, you see. Although I didn't agree with their philosophy, quite the opposite, I still felt we were their hosts. They'd asked to see us and I wanted to know what was going on in their minds.

Bonner was still laughing when, on the dot of one minute to ten, the Russians walked into my office. His face fell a mile. The police didn't even know that they'd left Ottawa and here they were in British Columbia, in my office.

What had they come for? One reason: to find out how we were able to handle our financial matters while the rest of Canada couldn't.

They came back year after year. We were frank with them and they were frank with us. For instance, I was the first to find out from them about the trouble they were having with China. I had taught Chinese students when I was a young man in Edmonton and had felt very close to them. I asked the Russians how they were getting along with the Chinese.

Through an interpreter, the one told me, "Funny you should ask that question, Mr. Premier, because we're not getting along at all well. They look upon us as barbarians. Their civilization is thousands of years older than ours, they tell us, and they're not going to follow us. We're having lots of trouble with them, lots of trouble."

Then they asked me about the United States. What would they do in this situation, would they make war?

I told them, "Don't make the big mistake. Don't make the mistake Napoleon and Hitler and those other people made. Don't even think that because a people say they're not strong enough to do this or that, they won't march when the time comes. They will march. The United States will march, Britain will march, France will march, they will all march even if they face sure defeat. Certainly, when we gave guarantees to Poland, we couldn't keep them, but we tried. We went to war with Hitler. Perhaps that was the saving of your own country, sir."

The Russian said to me, "We'll never make that mistake. We'll never go too far. We too have learned a few good lessons from history."

I was amazed at the discussions I had with them out here in little British Columbia, and how frank they could be. In fact, I still try to keep up with them. I've got a book called *The Russians* and I'm studying it. You've got to study every people, to find out what really makes them tick. What is behind the gloss? One must always ask: what is their real spirit?

~ 13 ~

Best for Canada

The elections of 1969 saw a fight between Bennett's government and a rejuvenated New Democratic Party. Although the Liberals barbecued gigantic mounds of spare-ribs and sunned themselves in the reflection of the charismatic Trudeau, they received no answering reality at the polls. The Tories fielded hardly any candidates.

For the election, the provincial NDP toppled Robert Strachan in favour of Tom Berger. The federal NDP airlifted organizers from Ontario, Saskatchewan and Manitoba, and when the results came in they wondered why they had bothered. Bennett garnered his highest percentage of the popular vote ever.

Berger was defeated in his own riding and handed over the leadership to Dave Barrett, a former social worker who had been fired from the civil service in 1960 for accepting the CCF nomination in Dewdney. In that election he had toppled Bennett's labour minister, Lyle Wicks.

Meanwhile, Pierre Elliot Trudeau sat in Ottawa with Gerard Pelletier and Jean Marchand, pondering how to sell federalism to fractious premiers such as W. A. C. Bennett. To them, Bennett and his kind stood in the way of a Liberally defined idea of national unity.

I NEVER WANTED to campaign for disunity. I only wanted unity. At all the federal–provincial conferences I attended I was forthright, saying what I thought was best for Canada as well as for British Columbia. In return, all I got was a reputation that I was anti-Ottawa. At no time was I opposed to the federal government except in that I was the number one enemy of centralism—then and always will be.

With centralism, you get central planning and in due course socialism, no matter what the party in power calls itself. You get a better kind of government if the power is spread around more.

For instance, if we had five distinctive regions in Canada, we'd be better off. Ottawa could keep certain basic jurisdictions, but these five autonomous regions, all within Canada, including Quebec, would each have the power that is now being used in Ottawa alone, only each region would use it for its own purposes. The result would be a more prosperous and a more united Canada.

I have a map here in Kelowna showing the five regions. Actually, I have a series of maps showing the expansion and the changes that occurred in Canada. I took the five-region map to a federal-provincial conference and showed it to everybody. Oh, but Trudeau and those other people were aghast. Why? Because they wanted to retain political power. They talk of unity but what they practise is disunity.

When they think of unity, they're like a father at the head of the table saying to his children "you do this and this and this." They keep all the control in their hands, everything has to be at the centre. But that makes for disunity. If you try to hold your sons too tight, you will lose them as they grow up. Let them expand, then you can't lose them. That's the way you build a family. It's the way you build a nation and it's the way you build the world.

Another idea I had concerned the federal government itself. Without Macdonald, there'd be no Canada. He set Canada up, but he didn't set it up on the proper basis at the time. When he made the second house, the Senate, it should have been similar to that of the United States. There should have been equal representation from every part of Canada. There should have been the same number of members in the Senate as in the Commons. The power would have rested in the Commons, as it should, but the Senate would have been a check on that power. It would have served Canadian unity so much better to have had equal representation from every province. Instead, we have this political patronage graveyard, call it what you like, of discarded politicians that in no way safeguards unity.

That's why I never sought membership in that house. I'm much too active to be a senator.

The new federalists in Ottawa launched their campaign with a well-publicized series of federal–provincial conferences. But all they achieved were murmurs of thanks from some of the provincial premiers and outright opposition from others, among them, W. A. C. Bennett.

A clash between him and Trudeau was almost inevitable. To Bennett, who had cut his teeth on economics and finance, Canadian Confederation was essentially a matter of economics. The nation's ears were now tuned to fine cultural distinctions as words such as "bilingualism" and "biculturalism" began to appear and pound their way into a generation's consciousness.

While Bennett had been building, Trudeau and his colleagues had been talking. In the waning hours of Duplessis' Quebec, they had developed a new concept of nationhood, of the French fact and of Canadian duality. Entering politics, they offered their ideas to the nation at large. Winning power, they put their theories into practice.

Bennett chose not to understand the thrust of the new arguments. He could see the federal cabinet being filled with French Canadians, and discerned only a distinct favouritism toward Quebec within Confederation. In fact, to him all this appeared as a new but parochial issue to keep the fires burning for Social Credit in British Columbia. He stumped the province, telling his listeners that they were now being governed from Quebec. His ministers attacked the Department of Regional Expansion, denouncing it for diverting funds to Quebec that were needed in Prince George or Prince Rupert. His roads maintenance men took down the federal Trans-Canada Highway signs, replacing them with ones that read "BC-1," a sentiment closer to Bennett's heart than language rights. Trudeau retorted by saying that Bennett was just "the bigot who happens to run the government there."

Sadly, with his predilection for the tangible, Bennett was

out of his element with slogans such as ecology, conservation, "the whole earth" and the Spirit of Woodstock. Nevertheless, he instinctively charged into battle with the New Federalism, only to find nothing solid to grasp. There were only words, and they were words that altered not things but human consciousness.

On the other hand, while it was true that Bennett had not taken much time to mull over the nuances of Canadian identity, he had given some serious thought to Quebec. Jean Lesage had been close to him, first as resources minister in the St. Laurent government, and then as the premier who started things moving in his own province. Bennett, having watched Lesage's performance, came to conclusions that were strikingly similar to those reached some years later by René Lévesque and his colleagues. But Ottawa would not listen to Bennett's views.

And there's the pity; for had Bennett's own vision, partisan as it may have been in part, meshed only partially with Trudeau's philosophy, alienation of the West may never have occurred.

To UNDERSTAND QUEBEC, you have to understand how Canada came into being. At one time Upper and Lower Canada—Ontario and Quebec—had trade arrangements with the United States which they then lost. Years later, Sir Wilfrid Laurier tried to get them back by proposing reciprocity. When I was a boy back in 1911, I disagreed with him, but he was right about reciprocity. We'd be in a much stronger position today if we had listened to him then. John A. Macdonald and George Étienne Cartier, representing Upper and Lower Canada, had lost the American market. They were looking around for others and saw the Maritime provinces as the only place where they could find additional markets. So they decided to bring them into Confederation.

Now, the Maritime provinces were holding a conference of their own in Charlottetown to discuss the joining together of Prince Edward Island, Nova Scotia and New Brunswick. Cartier and Macdonald went to Charlottetown and took these people by storm. The same year, they brought them to Quebec and together they made a start on Confederation. But the

Maritime provinces lost their prosperity because their natural
markets were with the New England states. They couldn't sell
to Central Canada.

Why did Upper and Lower Canada want them in Confederation? Why did they want to develop the West after that?
Why did they want a separate British North America apart
from the United States? Because they could be in the centre
controlling trade and manufacturing. They could have their
own large markets in Ontario and Quebec and ship goods east
to the Maritimes and west to the Prairies and British
Columbia. This would put them into a key position.

Now these facts have never been explained to Quebec.
Nobody has ever told Quebec that she has a key position totally
in the centre of Canada. It's a position that she will not be able
to hold on to if she separates from the rest of Canada.

What has happened is that a group of politicians, mostly
Liberals, have led Quebeckers by the nose. After the First
World War, for instance, I remember seeing billboards all over
the province showing Sir Arthur Meighen—a brilliant young
lawyer who had brought in the War Act during the war—
standing behind an ordinary citizen, blood dripping from his
hands. That's what they did, those Liberal politicians, they
stirred up the people. They planted seeds of discontent and
now they're reaping the whirlwind; but they were the ones
who planted them.

Quebeckers have never been shown the true picture—the
great advantages of being able to trade east and west, the benefits of the tariffs. You see, being in that central position,
they never had to pay heavy freight rates either. The East and
the West are the ones who have to pay heavy freight rates, not
Quebec.

Quebeckers never had explained to them how much they
receive through equalization payments from the federal
government—about $1 billion a year. British Columbia
doesn't get that much, Alberta doesn't get that much, nor does
Ontario, and so on. Quebeckers have been kept in the dark
about that too.

The federal government buys hundreds of millions of dollars worth of supplies, mostly from Ontario and Quebec. Quebeckers have never been told about that either.

In the past they've had poor management in Quebec, poor leaders, although some of them have been my friends. Premier Jean Lesage started the first reforms, but they were only temporary because he was stalled by lack of funds. When they needed sound financing, it wasn't Ottawa that helped them out, it wasn't Ontario or the others. It was British Columbia that loaned Quebec $100 million in 1964, on the strength of a handshake, with no written agreement and without security. I shook Lesage's hand, and he shook mine. I set the rate at 5.05 percent, and we agreed on the repayment dates. They kept their word, they paid it all off.

When I made the loan, I had no authority to do so from the people of British Columbia. If Quebec hadn't paid it back, my name would have been mud and I would have been driven from public life. But I did it to show that we, way off there on the Pacific coast, appreciated Quebec and had faith in her.

British Columbia has always understood Quebec, but Ottawa has never understood her. To retain power, the Liberals played Quebec against all the other provinces as if it were a political football.

To some, our $100 million loan might have looked like a gesture to preserve a united Canada. But it wasn't just a meaningless notion. I had confidence in them then and I still have it now. Take away this Liberal hierarchy and we can all come to a new Confederation.

I've always been in favour of unity; that's why I wanted Réal Caouette to be our national Social Credit leader instead of Robert Thompson. I thought Caouette would do a better job unifying Canada. He was a nationalist, a good Canadian, but also an imperialist who believed in the Queen. He was all the way down the street in favour of one united Canada. He told the same story in Quebec as well as in Vancouver. He was a very honest and forthright man; what more can you ask?

I've often been accused of attacking Ontario. I've done it

only because of centralism. I'd even attack British Columbia if she were the central force. To me, Ontario is an amazing province with amazing people. Like Quebec's, her location is wonderful; she can trade both ways and enjoy all the benefits of tariffs and freight rates. Surely, just pointing that out doesn't make you anti-Ontario. Nor am I jealous of Ontario; in fact, I'd like to see someone from there, the present premier or another great leader, head a movement to build a new Canada, based on a new Confederation. I think that leader should come from Ontario because that province has the respect of the Maritimes and the West, as well as of Quebec.

Let us not forget that above any campaign for a new Confederation stands the Queen. She transcends all the turmoil that exists in Canada now. The monarchy is basic to a united Canada; our whole political life is based on the monarchy. When Lévesque took the oath of office after he was elected premier, even though he had run as a separatist, he took it not to Ottawa, not to Canada, but to Her Majesty the Queen. Anything you do, you do in the name of the Queen.

Winston Churchill once said, "The British parliamentary system might be a terrible system, but tell me of any other system that's half as good." He also pointed out that if a premier or a prime minister wins a great majority, the people go out into the streets and shout "Long Live The Queen." But if the prime minister makes a mistake that is unpopular, the people go out into the streets and shout, "Kill the prime minister." The Queen is above all that.

~ 14 ~
On Moral Grounds

In 1972, Bennett rested his campaign against Ottawa to tour his province. In thirteen days, he covered over three thousand miles, touching fifty communities. From his chauffeured limousine, the premier and his entourage handed out scrolls, cufflinks and knick-knacks. In Kelowna he uncovered the crowning jewel in the diadem of his progress—the Kelowna Charter, a document that offered to repeal succession duties, increase benefits to old-age pensioners, students and the handicapped, and raise the minimum wage in the province.

But there was no thunder when that scroll was unrolled, no echoes ringing from the welkin. The charter crashed to the floor, but the thud failed to dismay Bennett. Just as Robert Bonner's departure in 1968 had gone unmourned and Dr. George Scott Wallace's defection in 1971, followed by Don Marshall's, had not caused tears to well up in Bennett's eyes, so he refused to be daunted by the charter's failure to stir the public. He decided to call an election.

Without issuing any warning to party faithfuls or to the opposition, he asked the press to meet him at the Hotel Vancouver. But now in 1972, there were others who sniffed the wind as keenly as the old man. One of them was Derril Warren, a bright, young lawyer who had become leader of an ever-reviving Conservative Party. He and several of his colleagues decided to stroll across to the hotel to see what the premier was up to.

Warren remained outside the room where Bennett had gathered the press, but he sent one of his people inside. His emissary soon returned to inform Warren excitedly that Bennett was calling an election. Warren, realizing that such an announcement would get Bennett's name into the evening papers ahead of his, had to act swiftly.

134

When a photographer from the Vancouver *Province* happened to wander by, Warren's people grabbed him, suggesting that if he wanted to get a good shot of the premier he had better stay outside the hotel room. Then Warren hid behind a column in the lobby, a point from which he could see the doors. When they opened and Bennett emerged, Warren sprang out from behind the column and rushed up to the premier with his hand extended. A preoccupied Bennett took Warren's hand and, believing him to be just another reporter, he shook it heartily. When he realized that he was shaking the hand of the young contender from the Conservative Party, a look of anger instantly crossed his face. As someone later observed, "it was a tremendous scowl." But the flash bulbs had popped and the scene had been recorded for the front pages of the evening paper. The pictures showed a tall, young and confident man, shaking hands with a snarling and aged premier.

Much later, someone confided to Warren, "Five or six years ago W. A. C. would have chewed you up and spit you out. He would have thrown his arm around your shoulders, pumped your hand and told the press that you were a nice young man but too young for politics."

During the campaign Bennett heard the cheers of hundreds along Main Street but sensed the silence of thousands beyond the bunting-strewn parade route. Twenty years before, Bennett had heard the tocsin of defeat sound for the government he had quit. Now he knew that Dave Barrett, leader of the NDP, was hearing the bells toll for the weary men who had followed Bennett.

Social Credit's message to the voters had become scrambled and slow, and Bennett knew it. But he had walked with fortune all the way. When her footsteps echoed in his mind as fortune left, he did not mistake the sound of his own feet for fortune's own—he knew his years of service were ending and those of the legend were about to begin.

WE LOST FOR MANY REASONS. I had been in power for many years longer than any other premier in British Columbia's history, over twenty years, in fact. The longest time before that was a British Columbia government in the early days under Sir Richard McBride, a Conservative who stayed for twelve years. All the other premiers were in for one, two, four or at most eight years, but never longer. And so the people thought that this government had been around long enough, perhaps too long.

Not only that, there had been a tremendous change in population. The people who were here originally knew what we had taken over and what Social Credit had done for the province. By then many of them had passed away and a lot of young chaps had grown up who did not know. Others who had come from all over the world had never known an under-developed British Columbia. And they just looked and listened to the call "time for a change." And then, I was getting old.

The other reason for our defeat was rising inflation. Inflation that could rob the people of their savings, of their homes, and of their pensions. I had studied all that around the world; I had studied British Columbia and how much inflation our economy and our production could stand—how much we could take without having inflation go wild. We arrived at a figure of 6.5 percent. Any person receiving money from the provincial taxpayer could not increase his or her wages or salaries by more than 6.5 percent a year. That was the most we could allow in the premier's salary, the MLAs' salaries, the civil servants' salaries. The teachers also were paid by the provincial government, and so were the doctors who received money under medicare.

I explained all that to the teachers. "You want 10 or 12 percent? That would be fine for you today, but what about thirty years from now? What about the young teachers starting out? What will happen to their pension funds? When you are young, do without a little now, and your pensions will be worth something in thirty years time. But if inflation goes wild, the money you have paid into these funds for thirty or forty years will be worth nothing. So you can have it now, or you can have it later." But they wanted it now, and they raised a fund of $1 million to fight us. These were the people who had been our friends.

And then there was the question of advertising liquor. I

was not opposed to liquor because I am a teetotaller. I recognize anybody's right to make his or her own choice. I certainly wasn't in favour of prohibition, but I had seen liquor ruin too many people, good ministers, good judges, lawyers, businessmen, travellers, and many, many more. I can see it ruining whole countries. In Russia, what is their problem? What is their problem in the great Scandinavian countries? Liquor! It is the Number One drug.

I had an act to put before the legislature which all the parties had supported. It was not in favour of prohibition, but to prohibit the advertising of liquor. We knew that sales wouldn't go down immediately, but perhaps in a few years they would start to decline and there wouldn't be any new customers. Nobody dared argue against that in the legislature, but the pressure was on everywhere.

I did the same thing with cigarette advertising, not because I didn't smoke. Everybody has the right to smoke if they want to, even if they know it's not good for them. But why subject people day in day out to pushers who promote smoking, showing a big business man at a social event, always with a cigarette in his hand? Why? Why?

We stopped the advertising, that's all. Now we had the powerful liquor and tobacco interests against us, as well as all the advertising people who had their accounts, and the newspapers, and the magazines. They didn't dare fight me openly, but they wrote editorials finding fault with a number of other petty little things.

The culmination was that we had been in there twenty years, long enough for any government really. I, the premier, was getting older; the population had changed; and we dared fight the powerful interests by opposing advertising of cigarettes and of liquor. We had attacked the money changers in the temples of cigarettes and liquor. We had to be defeated. "Anything but the Socreds, anything but the Socreds, anything but W. A. C.!" they cried.

I was sure that although the opposition would vote with us on the anti-advertising bills they would attack us as soon as we got into an election. "For the first time," I said to our cabinet, "I think we are facing defeat. We have to be defeated someday! What more glorious time to be defeated than after twenty years of a great track record! We have brought development, and we have fought for the things that were important. We have built roads and universities, and we brought in medicare. These are the great things. Let's fight the election on these moral issues—the sanctity of the individual. Don't help the young people destroy their lungs and bodies. When you see a brilliant young chap growing up who has the opportunity for a great future, would you make a drunk out of him? Nobody who started to drink socially ever wanted to become a drunk, but a large percentage of them end up being drunks. Don't be part of that. Let's fight this election on moral grounds. If we are defeated, we are defeated. You've got to put your record, your conscience and your beliefs on the line, and stand up and be counted. Because for the rest of your life you'll blame yourself for not having had the courage to do it, and for putting politics before high principles."

A good political leader is a person who really believes in what he does, who can inspire his lieutenants to go out and do things for the good of the people, things he might not have the courage or the insight to do alone.

I had the province in good shape financially; hundreds of millions of dollars were on hand, including millions and millions in special accounts using just the interest to finance good causes. We had a great hydro system, great universities, medicare, highways, everything, all had been completed.

Ours was known as "The Second Look Government." Some of the things we had approached may have led us onto the wrong road; so, early in our government I developed a policy that we would take a second look. A leader must not go ahead disregarding the new information that comes to him; he must be willing to take a second look.

How many people can stand up to all the problems and attacks that are bound to come to those who raise their heads above the crowds? People, newspapers and radio critics will always shoot at them.

In 1968, Philip Gaglardi was charged with misusing a government airplane, one we had rented. The plane was needed for him so that he could get around the whole province, as only the southern part was settled. He had to travel all over when he was minister of highways. Once he took a trip to the United States, and his daughter-in-law came along. The airplane had to come down to be serviced, anyway. Oh, they made a dreadful row about that. But as soon as the socialists got in, they acquired dozens of planes. And in Ottawa they have dozens of them, and what do they do? They fly their nannies across the ocean!

~ 15 ~

The Best
Fortune of All

After his defeat in 1972, Bennett retired to his home in Kelowna. There he found time to reflect on his years of achievement. In 1977, when these interviews were being taped, he celebrated his fiftieth wedding anniversary. Out of a special room came the commemorative trays, the medals and the souvenirs, there to be looked at with his family. And when the end came, he was with his family, the base from which he had worked during all those years, years that were made sunnier when, in 1975, his son Bill swept into power at the head of a rejuvenated Social Credit Party.

IF I'M TO BE REMEMBERED AT ALL, I'd like it to be as a leader, not for the classes, but for the masses. The traditional parties are government by classes. The Liberals and Conservatives are class governments, looking after big business and the powerful, who give them their campaign funds. The socialist governments are tools of big labour, who supply them with money to be able to call the tune. That's class government whether it's to the left or to the right.

I wanted to lead the development of our country, so that better social conditions and more benefits could come to the ordinary people. The rich and the powerful, be they labour or financial bosses, they can look after themselves. They *should* look after themselves. But who looks after the ordinary people? I would like to be known for having done that when I headed the government.

People thought I was a tough premier. I was the softest premier they ever had. I'm too emotional. Loyalty wasn't my weakness, but being emotional was; I was too soft.

Thank goodness the opposition never knew of my weakness. They would attack, attack, and attack me again and again and again. And the press would attack. That was just dandy for me because I just love a heckler. I love attack. I think, if they had praised me, I would have broken up. I'm a very emotional person.

Let me give you an example: there was a lady in Kelowna whose husband was a great big man, the best golfer around here; but he had a terrible temper. Usually he was out of a job, but whenever he had one he'd hit his boss on the second day and get himself fired.

This little lady had about seven children. She was very industrious and did the best she could for them. But, because her husband was usually unemployed, she was on welfare. The bureaucracy was always taking her off the welfare roll, and she'd come to me and I would always put her back on because I knew how much she was doing for her family. What effect would it have had on the public purse if she hadn't been helped a little to get over these bad patches in her life? The cost would have been ten times higher if she would have been allowed to go under.

When I retired from public life, she phoned me and told me about all her children and what they were doing. Every one of them had become a great success. On certain things we followed the hard line, but if somebody appealed to me personally, somebody who really needed help, I was the softest touch.

I never wanted to build a Bennett dynasty and I was pleased that my other boy, Russell, never went into politics. Everyone has two careers in life and some may have three. The first is your home life, the foundation of any other career you might have, the second is your business, and the third may be your political career.

But it is great for me to know that my son Bill has chosen to follow a political career. Before Bill entered politics, Russell, my other son, had more friends than Bill in the community and elsewhere. He could go anywhere, phone up anyone, no matter where he went around the world. Bill wouldn't; he was more abrupt. But he is perhaps the smartest person on figures that I've ever met. When he was seven or eight years old, he would read a book an hour. At nine, he was getting six books at a time out of the library. He'd use different names so he could get that many. But ultimately he developed a tremendous capacity for finance.

In business, the two boys could complement one another nicely. But when Bill entered politics—well I'm as positive as one can be that the two miss each other. Russell, that's R. J., can't call on Bill anymore because Bill is not allowed to have an interest in the business. All his assets are in a blind trust, and Russell looks after his own interests and those of his brother. And Bill cannot call on R.J.; he has to make decisions on his own.

I know what it's like. I'm a shy man myself. I'm actually bashful. But you forget about your shyness when you lose yourself in politics. You become so absorbed in what you are doing. If you don't you will always be self-conscious and achieve nothing. When I became a politician, I suddenly found out that I could address thousands of people and it wouldn't bother me one bit.

If it hadn't been for the quiet strength of my wife, I would never have been able to build up my business to the level where it is now. Nor would I have been able to raise a family as well as we managed to raise our family, or pursue the political career I have had.

My wife never spoke for me on a public platform, but she spoke for me in the way she lived. A lot of people would say, "We don't like that W. A. C., but he can't be all bad since he has such a wonderful wife, May." That didn't happen once, it happened hundreds and hundreds of times.

I admire her understanding, too. When we got married we had come to an agreement, for instance, that when we would differ on a subject, we wouldn't start a fight, but we'd withdraw from the discussion and present it again at a later time.

Somehow, she always tried to understand what I was trying to do and I always tried to understand her motives and opinions on pertinent questions. I can honestly say that we have never had a nasty argument in all the years we've been married.

I saw May's good qualities from the start. We had an understanding that she would run our home and I would run the business and the politics. I trust her and she trusts me. She never asked me about our finances, but she knew that I didn't want to go broke. I never had to tell her not to spend money here and there because I knew that she didn't want us to go broke either. Although we had some difficult years financially when we first started our married life, we never argued about money.

There may be a lot of people you like and they may like you; but I honestly believe a person falls in love genuinely only once in a lifetime. I think the greatest fortune for two people is when they fall in love with each other. That's the best fortune of all.

Bibliography

Friesen, J. and H. K. Ralston, eds. *Historical Essays on British Columbia.* The Carleton Library. Toronto: McClelland and Stewart Ltd., 1976.

Lipton, Charles. *The Trade Union Movement of Canada, 1827-1959* (3rd ed.). Toronto: NC Press Ltd., 1973.

Lower, Arthur J. *Canada on the Pacific Rim.* Toronto: McGraw-Hill Ryerson Ltd., 1975.

McGeer, Patrick. *Politics in Paradise.* Toronto: Peter Martin Associates Ltd., 1972.

Ormsby, Margaret. *British Columbia: A History* (rev. ed.). Toronto: Macmillan Co. of Can. Ltd., 1971.

Parker, Ian. "Simon Fraser Tolmie, the Last Conservative Premier of British Columbia," in *B. C. Studies*, Fall 1971.

Robin, Martin. *The Pillars of Profit, the Company Province, 1933-72.* Toronto: McClelland and Stewart Ltd., 1973.

Scott, A. D. "Introduction: Notes on a Western Viewpoint," in *B. C. Studies*, Spring 1972.

Sherman, Patrick. *Bennett.* Toronto: McClelland and Stewart Ltd., 1966.

Smiley, Donald. *The Rowell-Sirois Report.* The Carleton Library Series. Toronto: McClelland and Stewart Ltd., 1963.

Worley, Ronald. *The Wonderful World of W. A. C. Bennett.* Toronto: McClelland and Stewart Ltd., 1971.

Index